The Principles
of Descartes'
Philosophy

Benedictus De Spinoza

Translated from the Latin by
Halbert Hains Britan

Open Court
La Salle, Illinois 61301

Library of Congress Catalog Card Number: 74-3096

The Principles of Descartes' Philosophy

ISBN: 0-87548-053-5

TABLE OF CONTENTS

PREFACE OF DR. MEYER I

THE PRINCIPLES OF DESCARTES' PHILOSOPHY

PART I.

PROLEGOMENON 11
DEFINITIONS: THOUGHT, IDEA, SUBSTANCE, MIND, BODY,
    GOD, ETC. 20
AXIOMS 22
THE FUNDAMENTAL PRINCIPLE OF ALL KNOWLEDGE . . 23
AXIOMS TAKEN FROM DESCARTES 25
GOD'S EXISTENCE DEMONSTRATED 30
THE ATTRIBUTES OF GOD 41
WHATEVER IS CLEARLY CONCEIVED IS TRUE 46
OTHER ATTRIBUTES OF GOD 51
EXTENDED SUBSTANCE 54

PART II.

CONCERNING THE PHYSICAL WORLD.

DEFINITIONS 57
AXIOMS AND LEMMATA 60
THE ESSENTIAL NATURE OF MATTER 63
CONCERNING MOTION 69
GOD THE CAUSE OF MOTION 79
MOVING BODIES TEND TO MOVE IN STRAIGHT LINES . . . 81
THE IMPACT OF MOVING BODIES 87

PART III.

INTRODUCTION 107
A POSTULATE 109
DEFINITIONS AND AXIOMS 111
THE FIRST DIVISION OF MATTER 112

TABLE OF CONTENTS

APPENDIX.

THE COGITATA METAPHYSICA.

PART I.

PAGE

CHAPTER I. DIVISION OF BEING 115
CHAPTER II. ESSENCE, EXISTENCE, IDEA AND POWER EX-
PLAINED 120
CHAPTER III. THE TERMS NECESSARY, CONTINGENT, IM-
POSSIBLE AND POSSIBLE EXPLAINED 124
CHAPTER IV. CONCERNING DURATION AND TIME . . . 129
CHAPTER V. CONCERNING OPPOSITION, ORDER, ETC. . . . 130
CHAPTER VI. CONCERNING UNITY, TRUTH AND GOODNESS 131

PART II.

CHAPTER I. CONCERNING THE ETERNITY OF GOD . . . 139
CHAPTER II. CONCERNING THE UNITY OF GOD 142
CHAPTER III. CONCERNING THE GREATNESS OF GOD . . 143
CHAPTER IV. CONCERNING GOD'S IMMUTABILITY . . . 146
CHAPTER V. CONCERNING THE SIMPLICITY OF GOD . . . 148
CHAPTER VI. CONCERNING THE LIFE OF GOD 150
CHAPTER VII. CONCERNING THE UNDERSTANDING OF GOD 152
CHAPTER VIII. CONCERNING GOD'S WILL 156
CHAPTER IX. CONCERNING THE POWER OF GOD 159
CHAPTER X. CONCERNING CREATION 161
CHAPTER XI. CONCERNING THE CONCURRENCE OF GOD . . 168
CHAPTER XII. CONCERNING THE HUMAN MIND . . . 170

INTRODUCTION

This translation, undertaken at the suggestion of Professor George M. Duncan of Yale University, has been made from the Latin text of Vloten's and Land's *Benedict de Spinoza Opera*, 1895. A careful study of this work such as a translator must needs make has convinced me that more attention should be given to the early writings of Spinoza for the help they give in understanding his Pantheism. By this means, by seeing how his ideas followed naturally if not always quite logically, from personal factors, and from Descartes' philosophy, some of the most obscure points in his system of philosophy are materially elucidated and explained. But a historical or genetic study of any subject today needs no apology. The only remarkable thing about this is that so little attention has been given to this method of clearing up the obscurities of Spinoza's thought.

The work on Descartes' philosophy translated below, the earliest of all his writings, was published in 1663 under rather unusual circumstances. It was the only work to which Spinoza ever subscribed his name, and yet he warns us that we must not accept this as an expression of his own belief. The story of its composition and publication is as follows: Spinoza about the year 1662-3 had a pupil to whom he was teaching Descartes' philosophy, being at that time unwilling to impart his own opinions to any one except to a few of his special friends with whom he was accustomed to discuss his philosophical views. Well founded conjecture makes this pupil to be Albert Burgh, who, being in later years converted to the Roman Catholic faith, takes his former instructor severely to task for his heresies. Be this as it may, the fact remains that the *"Principles of Descartes' Philosophy"* was not meant to be an expression of Spinoza's own belief at the time it was written. Not wishing his own opinions to be known at that time he conceives the plan of teaching his pupil the philosophy of Descartes, which he could do conscientiously and without any unpleasant results to himself. This work was written, therefore, more to conceal than to express his own belief. Spinoza, as it seems, solely for the benefit of his pupil, had put the second part of the *Principles* in geometrical form. Some of his philosophical friends, seeing this, and being impressed with the *method* in which it was expressed asked him to put the first and third parts in the same form, and, appending the *Cogitata Metaphysica,* to permit the whole to be published. This Spinoza readily consented to do, if some one of them would go over the work perfecting the phraseology, and would write a preface explaining that this work was not meant to be an expression of his own belief, but that it was a faithful presentation of the philosophy of Descartes, either what he had said explicitly or that which could logically be inferred from his premises.

Thus we are forewarned lest we should accept the propositions given below as an expression of Spinoza's own thought. Some of the positions taken, we are told in this Preface, do express his own belief, but there are others to which he holds exactly the contrary opinion. We are not at liberty, therefore, to subscribe Spinoza's name to all that is said in this work but must sift out as best we can that with which he agreed from that which he rejected.

Dr. Ludwig Meyer, a physician in Amsterdam, and a man intimately acquainted with Spinoza's opinions, gladly agreed to write such a preface as Spinoza desired, and this is given as an introduction to the work in question. Spinoza immediately set to work and in two weeks' time had the first part also in geometrical form and sent it to be published with the rest. Another reason why he entrusted its publication to his friend was that he had left Amsterdam in 1660 on account of persecution and was at this time dwelling in Rheinsburgh, near Leyden. The following letter to Oldenburgh gives us his own version of the publication of the work:

Distinguished Sir:—

I have at length received your long wished for letter, and am at liberty to answer it. But before I do, I will briefly tell you what has prevented my replying before. When I removed my household goods here in April, I set out for Amsterdam. While there certain friends asked me to impart to them a treatise containing, in brief, the second part of the principles of Descartes treated geometrically, together with some of the chief points treated in metaphysics, which I had formerly dictated to a youth, to whom I did not wish to teach my own opinions openly. They further requested me, at the first opportunity, to compose a similar treatise on the first part. Wishing to oblige my friends I at once set myself to the task, which I accomplished in a fortnight, and handed over to them. They then asked leave to print it, which I readily granted on the condition that one of them should, under my supervision, clothe it in more elegant phraseology, and add a little preface warning readers that I do not acknowledge all the opinions there set forth as my own, in as much as I hold the exact contrary to much that is there written, illustrating the fact by one or two examples. All this the friend who took charge of the treatise promised to do, and this is the cause for my prolonged stay in Amsterdam. Since I returned to this village I have hardly been able to call my time my own, because of the friends who have been kind enough to visit me. At last, my dear friend, a moment has come when I can relate these occurrences to you, and inform you why I allow this treatise to see the light. It may be that on this occasion some of those who hold the foremost positions in my country will be found desirous of seeing the rest of my writings, which I acknowledge to be my own, they will thus take care that I am enabled to publish them without any danger of infringing the laws of the land. If this be as I think, I shall doubtless publish at once; if things fall out otherwise, I would rather be silent than obtrude my opinions on men, in defiance of my country, and thus render them hostile to me. I therefore hope, my friend, that you will not chafe at having to wait a short time longer; you shall then receive from me the treatise printed, or the summary of it you ask for. If meanwhile you would like to have one or two copies of the work now in the press I will satisfy your wish as soon as I know of it and of means to send the book conveniently.[1]

In obtaining a better translation for certain passages help has sometimes been found by consulting the standard Histories of Philosophy such as Erdmann's, Kuno Fisher's, and Ueberweg's as well as Torrey's and Veitch's translation of Descartes' works, and Elwes' translation of the earlier works of Spinoza. My thanks are also due to Professor Duncan for his suggestion upon some points, and to Professor C. R. Melcher of Hanover College for reading over a portion of my MSS.

HALBERT HAINS BRITAN.

Hanover, Indiana, January, 1905.

[1] Letter XIII. Elwes' Trans. Spinoza's Works.

LUDWIG MEYER

TO

THE WORTHY READER.

S. P. D.

It is admitted by all who have any claims to superior intelligence that the method of mathematics, viz., the method by which conclusions are demonstrated from definitions, postulates, and axioms is the best method of obtaining and imparting truth. And rightly so; for as certain knowledge of an unknown object can only be obtained through facts previously known, there must of necessity be certain premises on which the whole superstructure of human knowledge rests, provided it does not fall of its own weight, or succumb to some slight attack from without. No one who has paid any attention to the noble study of mathematics can doubt its definitions or postulates or axioms. For definitions are but a very open explanation of the terms and names under which the subject is discussed, and the postulates and axioms of mathematics, or the general ideas of the mind, cannot be denied by any one who understands the use of his vocabulary.

Nevertheless mathematicians are almost the only ones committed to such a method. Others employ a method radically different from this, namely, a method where the end is attained through definitions and logical division interspersed with numerous questions and explanations. For almost all believe, and many well informed persons have asserted that this method is peculiar to mathematics and should be abjured in all other branches of study. Therefore they, in their discussions, are unable to offer apodeictic proof, but are compelled to reason by analogy and from probable evidence. They produce a whole medley of ponderous volumes in which nothing is established with certainty, but which are full of contending views; what is in one place asserted is presently, and for a similar reason, denied. So much so that the mind eager for eternal truth, when it had hoped to find the tranquil expanse of its own desire, and crossing this with propitious speed to gain the haven of true cognition, finds itself on a tempestuous sea of thought tossed about and overcome, surrounded by storms of contending belief, and lost amid waves of uncertainty, without hope of rescue.

There are some, however, who, regretting this wretched plight of Philosophy, in order that they may leave to posterity some studies beside mathematics established with absolute certainty, have departed from the ancient method to this new path, arduous though it be. Some of these have put into literary form the philosophy now accepted and accustomed to be taught in the schools; others have set in order new systems elaborated through their own reflection. Although for years the task was undertaken in vain, at length that splendid star of our century Rene Descartes arose, who, after he had made clear the mathematical truth that was inaccessible to the ancients, and everything desired by his contemporaries, also discovered this fundamental principle of all knowledge. By means of this truth he was able to elaborate and establish many things with mathematical certainty. To any one who attends to his writings, which cannot be too highly praised, this will be as evident as the midday sun.

Although the philosophical writings of this incomparable man contain a method of demonstrating mathematics, it is not the method found in Euclid and in other geometries. Descartes' method, which he called *Analysis* and maintained was the best way to discover truth, was widely different from this. In the end of his "Response to the Second Objection," he recognizes two kinds of apodeictic demonstration. The one, *Analysis,* which he showed to be the true method, by which truth is discovered methodically and as it were *a priori;* the other by *Synthesis,* the method in which a long series of definitions, and premises and axioms, and theorems, and problems is used so that if anything is denied in the conclusion, it is immediately shown to have been contained in the premises. By this means assent is extorted from the reader however unwilling or unyielding he may be.

Granted, however, that truth may be established beyond all chance of doubt by these two methods, still they do not have an equal value. For many plainly unlearned in mathematical knowledge and so wholly ignorant of the method by which such truth is discovered (analysis), and by which it is set in order (synthesis), are not only unable to teach this truth to others but are unable to follow it for themselves. Whence it happens that many who have made his opinions and dogmas only a matter of memory, carried away by some thoughtless attack or influenced by the authority of others, have defamed the name of Descartes, and, when a discussion of these things arises, since they cannot demonstrate anything, garrulously repeat what has always been ascribed to the Peripatetic Philosophy. Wherefore, in order that this state of affairs might be improved, I have often desired that some one, alike skilful in Analysis and Synthesis, well versed in the writings of Descartes, and thoroughly master of his philosophy, might give his attention to this work and what he has put in analytic form remold in synthetic order and demonstrate in the more familiar forms of geometry. I myself, although fully conscious of my unfitness for that task, have often been inclined to undertake it. Other occupations, however, have filled my time and prevented me from acting on my desire.

I was very glad to know, therefore, that our author had put into geometrical form, for a pupil whom he was teaching Descartes' philosophy, the entire second Part of the *Principles* and a part of the third, together with some important questions and difficulties usually discussed in Metaphysics, and not yet discussed by Descartes; and that he had consented, at the urgent request of his friends, that these, corrected and revised by himself, should be published. I, therefore, approving this purpose, offered my services, if he had any need of them, in helping to publish the work. I asked and even urged him that he should put the first Part into similar form and let it precede the two already done, in order that the work might be complete and therefore more intelligible. Although for good reasons he did not wish to do this, he was unwilling to refuse his friends or to neglect anything which might be done for the benefit of the reader. He entrusted to my care the entire management of the publication since he had departed from the city into the country and was unable to be present.

This is what we offer you, therefore, dear reader, in this little volume: viz., the first and second Parts of Descartes' Principles of Philosophy, together with a fragment of the third, to which we have added under the name of an appendix the *Cogitata Metaphysica* of our author. But when we speak of the first Part of the Principles, and the title of the book suggests the same thought, we do not wish it understood that all that Descartes has said in this is here presented demonstrated in geometrical order, but only that preferable terms have been selected and those principles which Descartes treated in his Meditations, which relate more particularly to Metaphysics. Those matters which are only of logical interest, however, or which Descartes expressed for their historical value, he has omitted. That he might the more easily effect this end our author, so far as the order is concerned, has transposed almost all that Descartes had put into geometrical form in the end of his " Response to the Second Objection." This he did by placing all of Descartes' definitions first and by inserting propositions of his own; by placing the axioms not together with his definitions, but a part of them after the fourth proposition; finally by omitting those not needed and by changing the order so that they might more easily be understood. It did not escape the notice of our author that these axioms might be demonstrated in the manner of theorems (as Descartes also held, Postulate 7.) and might even properly be classed as propositions. We, indeed, urged him to do this, but the amount of work with which he was employed only left him two short weeks in which to complete the work. For this reason he was unable to satisfy his own and our desire, but merely adding a brief explanation in place of the demonstration, he postponed until another time the complete and perfected volume, if perchance after this imperfect edition a new one should be demanded. To this end we shall urge him to complete the third Part concerning the visible world. (Of this we have added the fragment our author had completed, for we were unwilling that the reader should be deprived of any part of his work, however small.) To better accomplish his purpose, certain propositions concerning the nature of fluid bodies had to be inserted in Part II. For my part, I shall urge him to speedily complete the work.

Not only in regard to the axioms, but also in demonstrating the propositions and in other conclusions our author often differs from Descartes; for example, the term apodeictic is used in a widely different sense. However, let no one think that he wished to correct that most illustrious man in these things, but only that he did this in order to retain the current order and not increase the number of axioms unduly. For this and for many reasons he was compelled to demonstrate many things which Descartes had stated without demonstration and to add much that he had omitted.

Nevertheless, I wish it to be noted first of all that in all of these Parts, viz., in the first and second Parts of the *Principles* and in the fragment of the third, as well as in the *Cogitata Metaphysica,* our author is merely expressing the opinions of Descartes with their demonstrations so far as they are found in his writings or as they logically follow from his premises. For when he promised to teach a pupil the philosophy of Descartes it was a matter of principle with him not to depart in the least from his opinions or to teach anything that did not follow from his dogmas, or was contrary to them. Wherefore, let no one think that he is teaching here his own opinions or only what he approves. Although he adjudges certain things to be true, he affirms that others are opposed to his belief. Many things he rejects as false, from which he holds a far different opinion. Of this nature, to mention only one from many, are those conclusions concerning the Will, Schol. Prop. 15, Part I., and Chapter 12, Part II. of the Appendix, although they seem to be proved with painstaking care. For he did not think that the Will was something distinct from Intellect, much less endowed with such freedom. For in these assertions, as is evident from his dissertation concerning method Part 4, *Meditation 2,* and in other places, Descartes merely affirms and does not prove that the human mind is an absolute thinking substance. Although our author indeed admits that there is a thinking substance in Nature, he denies that this constitutes the essence of the human mind. He believed that in the same way that there are no limits to Extension, so Thought is in no way determined. And as the human body is not absolute, but its extension is determined according to natural laws of motion and of rest, so also the mind or human spirit is not absolute but is determined through ideas by natural laws of thought. These, we ought to conclude are given when the body begins to exist. From this definition it is easy to show that the Will and the Intellect cannot be distinguished, much less, as Descartes affirmed, can we say that the Will is endowed with liberty. To say that it is the faculty of affirming or of denying is wrong, for to affirm or to deny is only a form of idea. Indeed, those faculties, as Intellect, Desire, etc., ought to be placed in the list of fictitious thoughts, or at least of those ideas which men have because of their powers of abstraction, as for example, with *humanity, lapidity,* etc.

Reference must also be made to another point which was prominent in the mind of Descartes, namely, *that this or that surpasses human knowledge.* For it must not be thought that our author states this as his own opinion. He believed that all these things, and even many things more subtle and more sublime, could not only be clearly and distinctly conceived by us, but even readily explained if only the human mind were led in the way which Descartes opened up and made possible for investigating truth and for acquiring knowledge. Therefore the principles of knowledge which Descartes set forth and the philosophy based upon these do not suffice for solving all those extremely difficult problems which relate to metaphysics, but others are required if we desire the intellect to sound the depths of cognition.

And finally, to bring our preface to an end, we wish the reader to know that these papers are published for no other purpose than to discover and to impart truth, and to incite in men a desire for a true and a sincere philosophy. So let every one, having been diligently warned, before he undertakes to read this work, determine to correct as far as possible certain typographical errors which have crept in, and to insert the omissions in order that he may receive the full benefit which we earnestly desire for every reader. For these obstacles, as any one can readily see, may easily prevent the force of the demonstration and the thought of the author from being easily seen.

AD LIBRUM.

Ingenio seu te natum meliore vocemus,
    Seu de Cartesii fonte renatus eas,
Parve Liber, quidquid pandas, id solus habere
Dignus, ab exemplo laus tibi nulla venit.
Sive tuum spectem genium, seu dogmata, cogor
    Laudibus Auctorem tollere ad astra tuum.
Hactenus exemplo caruit, quod praestitit; at tu
    Exemplo haud careas, obsecro, parve Liber;
    Spinozae at quantum debet Cartesius uni,
    Spinoza ut tantum debeat ipse sibi.

                        —J. B., M. D.[1]

[1] Probably by J. Bresser, M. D.

The Principles of Philosophy Demonstrated by the Method of Geometry.

PART I.

PROLEGOMENON.

Before giving these propositions and their demonstration it seems best to recall briefly why Descartes came to doubt all things, how he discovered the fundamental principle of all knowledge, and finally how he liberated himself from this universal doubt. All of this we would have put in mathematical order if we had not thought that such prolixity would have impeded our understanding of these things which should be seen as clearly as though presented in a picture.

In order to proceed with his investigation with the utmost caution Descartes was compelled:

1. To lay aside all prejudices.
2. To find the fundamental truth on which all knowledge rests.
3. To discover the cause of error.
4. To understand everything clearly and distinctly.

In order to accomplish the first three points he doubted all things, not, however, as a sceptic who doubts merely for the sake of doubting, but in order to free his mind of all prejudices, so that he might find at length the firm and certain truth on which all knowledge rests. By using this method, such a truth, if any such existed, could not escape him. For this principle must be so clear that it needs no proof, and cannot under any circumstances be doubted; every demonstration must presuppose it. Such a truth he found after a long period of doubt. And after he had once gained this truth it was not difficult to distinguish the true from the false, or to detect the cause of error. And thus he could be on his guard lest he accept anything doubtful and false for what is certain and true.

To accomplish the last point, viz., to understand everything clearly and distinctly, his principal rule was to examine separately all the simple ideas from which all others are composed. For when he clearly and distinctly understood these simple ideas, he was enabled to understand in the same thorough way, all others into which they entered as component parts. Having prefaced our remarks with these few words we shall proceed with our purpose as stated above, namely, to explain why he doubted everything, how he found the fundamental truth of all knowledge, and how he extricated himself from the difficulties of these doubts.

Concerning his universal doubt. In the first place he calls attention to all of those things perceived through the senses, the heavens, the earth and all external objects. So also, even concerning those things which he thought to be most certain he doubted, because he knew that his senses had sometimes deceived him, and in sleep he had often persuaded himself that many things existed in which he later found he had been deceived. And finally because he had heard competent witnesses affirm that they sometimes felt pain in limbs recently lost. It was not without reason, therefore, that he doubted everything even the existence of his own body. Hence from all these reasons he was able to conclude that sense perception is not a certain foundation for knowledge (all that the senses give may well be called in doubt), but certainty rests upon some more indubitable principle than this. To investigate further he next notices the universal attributes of corporeal matter, as extension, form, quantity, etc., as well as all mathematical truth. Although these seem more certain than the objects of sense perception, nevertheless, he finds a cause for doubting them as well. Some err even in these, and beside there is an old idea that God, who is omnipotent, and has created us with our present faculties, has perhaps so made us that we are deceived even in those things which seem most certain. These are the causes that led him to doubt all things.

The discovery of the fundamental principle of all knowledge.

In order to find the fundamental truth in knowledge, he afterward inquired whether all things which are subjects of cognition could be doubted, if perchance there was anything which he had not yet called in question. Doubting in this way he believed that if anything was found, which, for none of the reasons given above, should be doubted, this might be considered the foundation on which all knowledge rests. And although, as it now seemed he had doubted everything (for he had called in question all that the senses give, and all that comes from the understanding), there was something left the certainty of which had not been doubted, namely, he himself who was doubting. Not, however, so far as he consisted of head or hands or other bodily members, for he had doubted the existence of these, but even while he was doubting he was thinking, etc. Carefully examining this fact he found that for no reason whatever could it

be doubted, for, whether waking or sleeping, if thinking at all he must therefore exist. And even though he
and others might fall into error, since they were in
error they must exist. Nor could he conceive of a
creator so skilful in deceit that he could deceive him
about this truth. For if it is supposed that he is deceived, it must also be supposed that he exists. Finally, whatever reason for doubt may be conceived, there
is none which does not at the same time make one more
certain of his own existence. Indeed the more arguments that can be assigned as cause for doubt the more
there are which convince him of his own existence.
So true is this that whoever begins to doubt will nevertheless exclaim, "*I doubt, I think, therefore I am.*"

In this truth he finds the ground of all knowledge
as well as the measure of all other truth, viz., *Whatever is as clearly and distinctly perceived as this is true.*

That nothing but this *Cogito ergo sum* can be the
fundamental truth in all knowledge is evident from
what has already been said. Concerning this it should
be noted in the first place, that it is not a syllogism
in which the major premise is omitted. If it were,
the premise *cogito* ought to be better known than the
conclusion, *ergo sum.* And if this were so the *ergo
sum* would not be the foundation of all knowledge.
Beside it would not be a certain conclusion, for its
truth depends upon universal premises which the
author had called in question. Therefore *Cogito ergo
sum* is one proposition equivalent to the statement
ego sum cogitans.

To avoid confusion hereafter (for the matter ought
to be thoroughly understood), we must know what
we are. For if I clearly understand this our essence

will not be confused with other things. To deduce this from what precedes our author thus proceeds:

He now recalled all those opinions formerly held, as for example, that his mind was something very fine in texture, like the wind, or fire, or air, interplaced with the coarser particles of the body; and that his body was better known than his mind and could be more clearly perceived. These opinions he now saw were at variance with what he had discovered. For he could doubt the existence of his body, but not his reality so far as he was a thinking being. Beside this, the body could not be clearly and distinctly known and therefore, according to his own dictum, should be rejected as non-existent. Therefore, since the body cannot be accepted as pertaining to his essence, so far as it is known, he further inquires what there is about his being which compels him to believe in his own existence. Such things were these: *that he had determined to be on his guard lest he be deceived; that he had desired to understand so many things; that he had doubted everything he was not able to know; that he had affirmed only one thing at a time; that he had denied all else, and even rejected it as false; that he had conceived many things though reluctantly; and finally that he had considered many things as though derived from the senses.* Since his existence was so evidently bound up with each one of these actions, and since none of them belonged to the things which he had doubted, and finally since they all may be considered as forms of thought, it follows that these are all true and pertain to his nature. So when he said *cogito* these modes of thought were all implied, viz., *to doubt, to understand, to affirm, to deny, to wish, to be unwilling, to imagine,* and *to feel.*

Some distinctions must here be noted that will have importance when we come to discuss the distinction between mind and body. (1) That modes of clear and distinct thought may be known even when some things are still in doubt. (2) That we render a clear and a distinct concept obscure and confused when we ascribe to it something concerning which we are still in doubt.

His liberation from doubt. Finally, in order that he might be certain and remove all doubt from those things he had called in question, he further proceeds to inquire into the nature of a perfect Being and whether such a Being exists. For when he has discovered that this Being, by whose power all things are created and preserved and to whose nature it would be repugnant to be a deceiver, exists, then he has removed that reason for doubt which is found in the fact that he was ignorant of the cause of his existence. For he knew that the power of discerning the true from the false would not have been given to him by a God of perfect goodness and truth in order that he might be deceived. Mathematical truth, therefore, and all other of like certainty cannot be doubted. To remove other causes for doubt he inquires next why it is we sometimes fall into error. For when he discovered how error arose, and that we use our free will to assert what we perceive only confusedly, he concluded straightway that we could avoid error by withholding assent from that which is seen only indistinctly.

As every one has the power of inhibiting the will he can easily restrain it to the limits of the understanding. And since in youth we form many prejudices from which we free ourselves only with difficulty, he

enumerates and examines separately all of our simple
ideas to assist us in casting these prejudices aside.
His object was to determine what was clear and what
was obscure in each. Thus he was able to distinguish
the clear from the obscure and to form clear and distinct ideas. By this means he easily found the real
distinction between mind and body; what was clear
and what obscure in those ideas derived from the
senses; and finally how sleep differs from waking.
When this was done he could doubt no longer concerning the waking life, nor could he be deceived by his
senses. In this way he was able to free himself from
all his recent doubt.

Before I close this part of the discussion it seems
that some satisfaction should be given to those who
argue, that since it is not known that God exists *per se*
it is impossible for us ever to know that God does exist.
For from uncertain premises (and we have said that
all things are uncertain so long as we are ignorant of
our origin), nothing can be concluded with certainty.

In order to remove this difficulty Descartes responded in this fashion; although we do not know
whether the creator of our nature has created us so
that we are deceived in those things which seem most
certain, nevertheless, we cannot doubt those things
we understand clearly and distinctly, so long as we
attend merely to them. But we only doubt those
things previously demonstrated, and now recalled to
memory, when we no longer attend closely to the
reasons from which they were deduced, which perchance are even forgotten. Therefore, though we
cannot know directly that God exists, but must learn
this by deduction, still, we are able to know this certainly, provided we attend very accurately to the prem-

ises from which the conclusion is deduced. Vid. Prin. Pt. I. Art. 13, and Response to Second, Obj. No. 3, and end of Med. 5.

But since this reply is not sufficient we will offer another. We saw above, when speaking of the evidence and certainty of our existence, that this was found in the fact that, consider what we will, we meet no argument for doubt which does not at the same time convince us of the certainty of our existence. This is true whether we consider our own nature, or conceive of God as a skilful deceiver, or adduce some extraneous reason for doubt. For example, considering the nature of a triangle, though we are now compelled to believe that its three angles are equal to two right angles we are not forced to the conclusion that this is really true if perchance we are deceived by our Creator. In the same way we deduce the certainty of our existence. We are not compelled to believe that under any conditions the three angles of a triangle are equal to two right angles. On the contrary we find reason for doubt, for we have no idea of God which compels us to believe that it is impossible for God to deceive us. It is equally easy for one who has no true conception of God to think that he is a deceiver or that he is not. So for those who have no right conception of a triangle it is equally easy for them to think that the sum of the angles is equal to two right angles, or that it is not. Therefore, we grant that we cannot be absolutely certain of anything except of our own existence, however closely we attend to the proof, until we have a clear concept of God which compels us to affirm (in the same way that the concept of a triangle compels us to affirm that the sum of its angles is equal to two right

angles) that he is perfectly true in His being. But
we deny that we are unable to come to any certain
knowledge of the external world. For, as now appears, the whole matter hinges upon this, viz., whether
we can form such a concept of God that it is not as
easy for us to think of Him as a deceiver as to believe
that He is perfectly true in His being. When we
obtain such a concept as this, all cause for doubting
mathematical truth is removed. For, when we consider how the doubt of this affects our own existence,
if we doubt this still we ought not to even affirm our
own existence. If now having obtained this concept
of God we consider the nature of a triangle we are
compelled to affirm that the sum of its three angles *is*
equal to two right angles; or if we consider the nature
of God, and this also compels us to affirm that He is
perfectly true and the author and continual preserver
of our being, we are not deceived. Nor is it less impossible for us to think when we once have obtained
this idea of God (which we suppose to be already
found), that He is a deceiver, then when we consider
the nature of a triangle to think that the sum of its
angles is not equal to two right angles. As we can
form such an idea of a triangle although we are not
certain that God is not deceiving us, so we can form
this idea of God, although we do not know whether
or not He is deceiving us. And, provided only that
we have such an idea of God, however it may have
been obtained, it is sufficient to remove all doubt.

This point having been made clear I shall remark
upon this difficult proposition: we can be certain of
nothing not merely as long as we are ignorant of God's
existence (for I have not yet spoken of this), but as
long as we do not have a clear and a distinct idea of

His being. Hence if any one should desire to oppose our conclusions, his argument should be as follows: We cannot be certain of anything so long as we have no clear and distinct idea of God. But we cannot have a clear and a distinct idea of God as long as we do not know whether or not he is deceiving us. Therefore we cannot be certain of anything as long as we do not know whether or not our Creator is deceiving us, etc. To this I reply by conceding the major premise but, denying the minor. For we have a clear and a distinct idea of a triangle although we do not know whether or not God is deceiving us. And in the same way we have a clear and a distinct idea of God as I have already shown, and, therefore, cannot doubt His existence, nor any mathematical truth.

Our prefatory remarks being thus completed we proceed now to the main problem.

DEFINITIONS.

I. *Under the term* thought *(cogitatio) I comprehend all mental phenomena of which we are immediately conscious.*

Thus volition, understanding, imagination and sense perception are all forms of thought. I have added the term *immediately* to exclude phenomena which directly depend upon and follow from these mental states. Thus voluntary motion arises as the direct result of some form of thought but is not itself a mental state.

II. *By the term* idea *(idea) I understand any form of thought of which we are conscious through immediate perception.*

I cannot express anything in words, therefore, with-

out thus making it certain that I have some idea which
these words are meant to signify. Therefore I would
even call the images depicted in phantasy, ideas, not,
however, so far as they are corporeal, i. e., as they
affect some portion of the brain, but only so far as
they affect the mind in that portion of the brain.

III. *By the* objective reality of an idea, *I understand the object represented by the idea.*

In the same manner I may speak of objective perfection, or of an objective art, etc. For whatever we
perceive in the objects of our ideas are objective in
the ideas themselves.

IV. *These characteristics are said to be* formally
(formaliter) *contained in the objects of our ideas
when they really are just as we perceive them. They
are said to be* eminently (eminenter) *contained when
they are not just as we perceive them but so great that
they can easily supply what we perceive.*

Note that when I say a cause *eminently* contains the
perfection of its own effect, I mean that the cause
contains the perfection of the effect more completely
than the effect itself. Vid. Ax. 8.

V. *Every object to which belongs as to a subject,
some property, or quality, or attribute, or through
which some things which we perceive exist, or of which
we have some real idea is called* substance.

Properly speaking, indeed we have no other idea
of substance than that it is an object in which either
formally or eminently something else exists which we
perceive, or that it is objective in something apart
from our ideas.

VI. *Substance in which thoughts are immediately
present, is called* mind.

I use the term *mind* (mens), rather than *spirit*

(animus), for the latter term is equivocal, often being used to mean a corporeal object.

VII. *Substance, which is the immediate subject of extension, and of accidents, which presupposes forms of extension as figure, position, and motion, etc., is called* body (corpus).

Whether mind and body are one and the same substance will be inquired into later.

VIII. *Substance which we know to be perfect in the highest degree, and in which nothing can be conceived implying a defect or limitation, is called* God.

IX. *When we say that something is contained in the nature of the thing itself or in its concept, it is the same as to affirm that this is true.*

X. *Substances are said to be distinct when the one can exist alone and apart from others.*

We have here omitted the Postulates of Descartes because we were unable to deduce any conclusions from them in what is to follow. Nevertheless, we earnestly ask the reader that he does not fail to carefully read them over and give them his earnest attention.

AXIOMS.

I. The knowledge and certainty of an unknown object depends upon the cognition of objects previously known.

II. There are reasons for doubting the existence of our own bodies.

(This was shown in the Prolegomenon, so may be placed here as an axiom.)

III. If our being comprises anything beside mind and· body it is not so well known as these.

(These axioms, it should be noted, do not affirm

objective existence, but only deal with objects as a part of our mental life.)

PROPOSITION I.

We cannot be absolutely certain of anything until we know that we really exist.

DEMONSTRATION.

This proposition is self-evident. For he who does not know that he exists, cannot know that he is affirming or denying. It should be noted, too, that although we affirm and deny many things that have no reference to our existence, nevertheless unless this fact is accepted as indubitable all things are in doubt.—Q. E. D.

PROPOSITION II.

The proposition ego sum *is self-evident.*

DEMONSTRATION.

If you deny that it is self-evident, it can be known only through some truth, prior to the proposition *ego sum* (per. Ax. 1), which is absurd (per Ibid.). Therefore it is self-evident.— Q. E. D.

PROPOSITION III.

The primary truth is not that I am a corporeal being, neither is this fact self-evident.

DEMONSTRATION.

There are some reasons for doubting the existence of our bodies (Vid. Ax. 2). Hence (per Ax. 1) we must derive this truth through something previously and more indubitably known. Therefore, the primary truth is not that I am a corporeal being nor is this fact self-evident.— Q. E. D.

PROPOSITION IV.

Ego sum *is the primary fact in cognition only so far as I am a thinking being.*

DEMONSTRATION.

The assertion that I am a corporeal being is not the primary fact in cognition (per Prop. III.) ; neither am I certain of my existence except as I am mind and body. For if I comprise in my being any thing beside mind and body, it is not so well known to me as body (per Ax. 3). Therefore *ego sum* is the primary fact of cognition only so far as I am a thinking being. —Q. E. D.

COROLLARY.

From the last proposition it is evident that the mind is better known than the body. (For a fuller explanation, see Art. 11 and 12, Part I. of the *Principles*.)

SCHOLIUM.

Every one is certain that he affirms, he denies, he doubts, he understands, he imagines, etc., or that he is a doubting, an understanding, an affirming—in a word—a thinking being. This truth no one can doubt. Therefore the proposition *cogito,* or *sum cogitans,* is the fundamental truth of all Philosophy. And, since for certain knowledge nothing more can be demanded or desired than that we deduce all things

from certain premises so that all our conclusions are
as certain as our premises, it follows that all that we
deduce from our principle so that if we doubt the
conclusion we must also doubt the premises, must be
held to be perfectly true. In order to proceed as
cautiously as possible, in the beginning I shall admit
to be of equal certainty only those things which we
perceive in ourselves so far as we are thinking beings.
As, for example, that one desires this or that, that one
has certain ideas, and that one thing contains more perfection than another; namely, that which contains objective perfection of substance is far more perfect
than that which contains only objective perfection of
some accident. Finally, that that is the most perfect
substance which contains the highest degree of perfect
being. These things, I say, are not only all as clear
as our first principle but, perhaps, are even more certain. For they not only affirm that we think but that
we think in this particular way. And we shall find,
when we come to test them, that they are not only
indubitable, but that we cannot doubt their verity
without doubting the fundamental truth of all knowledge. For example, if some one should say he is in
doubt whether something can arise from nothing, he
might also doubt his own existence even when he is
thinking. For if I can affirm that something can exist
without a cause I can, by the same right, affirm that
thought may exist without a cause and that I think
although I am nothing. Since this is impossible I
cannot believe that something can arise from nothing.
Leaving these matters for the present, it seems necessary, in order to proceed, to add to the number of
Axioms we have already given. In the end of his
" Response to the Second Objection," Descartes has

given certain truths as axioms, and I could not wish
to be more accurate than he. Nevertheless, in order
to preserve the order now begun, and to render them
a little clearer, I shall attempt to show how they depend one upon the other and all upon the principle
Ego sum cogitans, or that they are all as certain as
this truth.

AXIOMS

Taken from Descartes.

IV. There are different degrees of reality or being.
For substance has more reality than accidents or mode;
and infinite substance than finite. So, too, there is
more objective reality in the idea of substance than in
the idea of accident; and in the idea of infinite substance than in the idea of finite substance.

*This axiom is known as true from a consideration
of those ideas of which we are certain because they
are modes of thought. For we know how much
reality or perfection the idea of substance affirms of
substance and how much the idea of mode affirms of
mode. And since this is true we know that the idea
of substance contains more objective reality than the
idea of its accidents, etc. (Vid. Schol. Prop. 4).*

V. A thinking being, if it were possible, would
immediately add to itself any attribute of perfection in
which it was lacking.

*Every one observes this in himself so far as he is
a thinking being; therefore (per Schol. Prop. 4) we
know that this is true. And for the same reason we
are equally certain of the inference.*

VI. In the idea or concept of everything, existence

either as possible or necessary is contained (Vid. Axioms of Descartes, No. 10).

In the concept of God or an absolutely perfect being, existence is necessary. For otherwise it would be imperfect which is contrary to the hypothesis.

VII. No object or quality of an object already existing can exist without some existing object as the cause of its existence.

In the Scholium to Prop. 4 I have shown that this axiom is equal in truth to the proposition Ego sum cogitans.

VIII. Whatever reality or perfection an object contains, this exists either formally (formaliter) or eminently (eminenter) in its primary or adequate cause.[1]

By the term eminently I mean that the cause contains the perfection of the effect more fully than the effect itself. By the term formally I mean that the cause and the effect contain the perfection to a like degree.

This axiom depends upon the previous ones. For if it is supposed that there is less perfection in the cause than in the effect we have a result without a cause, and this is absurd (per Ax. 7).

Therefore nothing can be the cause of a given effect except that in which is contained eminently or at least formally, all the perfection found in the effect.

IX. The objective reality of our ideas requires a cause in which this same reality is not only objectively contained, but one in which it is found formally, or eminently.

Although this axiom is evident to all, many misuse it. For when some one forms some new idea everyone wishes to know why he did so. When they can

[1] Cf. Veitch's Descartes, p. 268, and Note p. 281.

assign some cause that contains formally or eminently all the perfection found in the concept they are content. Descartes has sufficiently explained this in his example of a machine (Vid. Prin. of Phil., Pt. I., Art. 17). So also if one inquires from whence man derives the ideas of his own thought and body, he finds that they are derived from himself. He discovers that he formally or at least constantly contains all that these ideas objectively contain. Therefore if one has some idea which contains more objective reality than he himself contains, impelled by reason he would seek some other cause outside of himself which formally or eminently contains all the perfection he is seeking to understand. Nor would any one ever assign any other reason for doing this than that he had conceived this with equal clearness and distinctness and that he had comprehended the truth of this axiom as it depends directly upon those preceding it. Namely (per Ax. 4), different degrees of reality or being are given in our ideas; and (per Ax. 8) for these degrees of perfection, some cause with equal perfection is required. But since these degrees of reality in our ideas are not merely in thought, but represent something in substance and its modes, in a word, so far as they are considered as images of things, it clearly follows that no other cause for this can be assigned than that all the reality they objectively contain is contained either formally or eminently in reason. This we have shown above and it is evident to all.

In order to make this perfectly clear I will illustrate with one or two examples. If one should see two books (for example, one written by a great philosopher and another by an uncultured man) written in the same hand, and should consider not the meaning of the

*words, i. e., the mental images they represent, but only
the delineation of the characters in which the thoughts
are expressed, he would discover no dissimilarity. So
he would not be led to look for different authors for
the books but would believe they were written by
the same person and with a common end in view.
But attending not to this but to the meaning of the
words and of the discussions he would find great differences, and would conclude that they certainly had
a different origin. He would find that the sense of
the words being considered, that is, the concepts they
represent, the one is far more perfect than the other.
I speak here of the first cause of the books. Although
as is evident the one might even have been derived
from the other.*

*We may illustrate further by the statue of some
leader. Here, if we attend only to the material used
we will find no cause for seeking a different sculptor for
this, and for some copy. Indeed, nothing hinders us
from thinking that the first is a copy of the second,
this again of a third and so on ad infinitum. If the
material alone is considered we do not need a separate cause for each. But if we consider the statue as
a statue we are immediately compelled to seek a first
cause which contained either formally or eminently
all that is presented to us. I do not see that this
axiom requires any further elucidation or confirma-
tion.*

X. No lesser cause is required for the conservation
of an object than for its first creation.

*Because at the present time we are thinking it does
not at all follow that we must continue to think. Our
concept of thought does not contain nor involve necessary existence. For I can clearly conceive of thought*

although I suppose that it does not exist. (This every one knows from his own experience so far as he is a thinking being). But since the nature of any cause ought to contain and involve in itself the perfection of its effect (per Ax. 8), it follows that there is something in ourselves or without us (as yet we do not know which) whose nature involves necessary existence. And this something is the primary cause of our thought both of its beginning and its continuance. For, although our thought began to exist, its nature and essence does not imply a necessary existence any more than it did before it began to be. It is therefore preserved in its existence by the same force that determined that it should exist. What we here affirm of thought is true also for every thing whose essence does not involve a necessary existence.

XI. Nothing exists of which we may not ask, what is the cause (or reason) of its existence. (Vid. Ax. I. of Descartes).

If anything positive exists we cannot say that it exists without a cause (per Ax. 7). Therefore we must assign some positive cause for its existence. This may be external, i. e., some cause outside of the object itself, or internal, i. e., something comprehended in the nature and definition of the object.

FOUR PROPOSITIONS TAKEN FROM DESCARTES.

PROPOSITION V.

God's existence is known merely from the consideration of his nature.

DEMONSTRATION.

It is equivalent to saying that a thing is true to say that it is contained in its nature or in its concept.

(per Def. 9). The concept of God includes necessary existence. Therefore it is true to say that he has a necessary existence in Himself, or that He exists. — Q. E. D.

SCHOLIUM.

Many important truths follow from this proposition. Indeed upon this truth alone, namely, that existence belongs to the nature of God, or that the concept of God involves a necessary existence as that of a triangle that the sum of its angles is equal to two right angles, or again that His existence and His essence are eternal truth, depends almost all our knowledge of God's attributes by which we are led to a love of God (or to the highest blessedness). Therefore it is extremely desirable that the human race should sometime consider this. I confess that there are certain prejudices which make this truth hard to see. But if any one with earnest purpose, impelled by the love of truth and its utility, wishes to examine into this, we recommend that he consider what is given in Meditation V. and in the end of his "Response to the Sec. Obj.," and also, what we have said of Eternity in Ch. I. Pt. II. of our Appendix. He would then understand very clearly, nor could he doubt that we do have an idea of God which is indeed the foundation of human blessedness; he would see clearly that the idea of God differs greatly from that of other objects; He would see, when he understands the essence and existence of God, that he differs *toto genere* from all other things. But there is no need to detain the reader longer.

PROPOSITION VI.

The existence of God may be demonstrated A POS-
TERIORI *from this, viz., that we possess this idea of
such a Being.*

DEMONSTRATION.

The objective reality of anything requires a cause
apart from our ideas, in which cause this reality is
not only objective, but in which it is contained either
formally, or eminently (per. Ax. 8). We have the
idea of God, and the objective reality of this idea
as it is not in our minds either formally or eminently
cannot be anywhere but in God himself. Therefore
this idea of God as we have it requires God for its
cause and He, therefore, exists.

SCHOLIUM.

There are certain ones who say they have no idea
of God, although, as they affirm, they love and worship
him. And although you place before their eyes the
definition and attributes of God, you have accomplished nothing. No more, by Hercules, than if you
should attempt to teach a man blind from birth the
different colors as we see them. Indeed, we ought
to give their words very little attention unless we wish
to consider them as a new species of animal half way
between man and the lower beasts. In what way
do I attempt to set forth the idea of anything except
by giving a definition and explaining its attributes?
Indeed when we are discussing the idea of God, it is
not so much that men deny the words as that they
are unable to form some image corresponding to these
words.

Then it should be noted that Descartes when he cites Axiom 4 to show that the objective reality of the idea of God is not in us either formally or eminently, supposes that every one knows that he is not infinite substance nor perfect in knowledge or power, etc. This he was justified in doing, for whoever thinks at all knows that there are many things he does not understand clearly and distinctly, and that he is even in doubt in regard to much that he sees.

Finally it should be noted that there are not many gods, as clearly follows from Axiom 8, but only one as we have shown in Proposition II. of this part and in Pt. II., Chapter II., of our Appendix.

PROPOSITION VII.

The existence of God is demonstrated in the fact that we, having the idea of existence, also exist.

SCHOLIUM.

To prove this proposition Descartes laid down two axioms, viz., (1) " Whatever is able to do that which is more difficult is able to do that which is less so. (2) It is greater to create or (per Ax. 10) conserve substance than attributes or properties of substance." What he meant by these I do not know. For these terms are not used absolutely but only in respect to a definite cause.[1]

So one and the same thing at the same time, in respect to different causes may be easy or difficult. If you call that difficult which requires more exertion,

---

[1] If you wish an example, consider the spider which easily spins its web, but for man this would be almost impossible. On the other hand, men easily do many things which perhaps are impossible for angels.

and that easy which requires less in the same case, as for example, the force which sustains fifty pounds could sustain twenty-five with double ease, clearly the axiom would not be true; neither does it demonstrate what he intended it should. For when he said, "If I have the power of preserving myself I have the power also of giving to myself all the works of perfection which I lack" (for that would require only as great power); I would concede that this energy used for self-preservation might be able to do many other things far more easily if I did not need it for conserving myself. But so long as I use this energy for self-preservation, I deny that it is possible to use it for accomplishing other things, though they be never so easy. This is clearly evident from our example. Nor does he take away the difficulty by saying, that as I am a thinking being I shall know this necessarily, for I employ all my strength in preserving myself which is the reason I do not give myself the attributes of perfection which I lack. For (although we are not now discussing this, but only how the necessity of this proposition follows from this axiom) if I know this I would be greater and perhaps would require, for preserving myself in such perfection, greater power than I now possess. And then I do not know that it is any greater task to create (or to conserve) substance than attributes, i. e., to speak clearly and more philosophically, I do not know but that substance requires all the virtue and essence by which it conserves itself, to conserve its attributes. But we leave this and will inquire, as this worthy author intended we should, into what is meant by the terms "easy" and "difficult." I do not think that by any means I could persuade myself that he understood by the term "difficult " that which is impossible (and so could not be conceived as existing), and by the term "easy" that which implies no contradiction (and so is easily conceivable). Although in the *Third Meditation* and in the observation he seems to mean that when he says: "Nor ought I to think that those things which are wanting in my nature are more difficult to acquire than the powers which I now possess. For, on the contrary, it is manifestly far more difficult for me as a being or a thinking substance to arise from nothing than, etc." For this is not in keeping with the words of the author nor consonant with his ability. And, indeed, though for the present I shall overlook it, between the possible and the impossible, or between that which is conceivable and inconceivable there is no relation, just as there is none between something and nothing. Power does not quadrate better with that which is impossible than creation and generation with non-being; such terms are not capable of relationship. Beside this it should be remembered that I can compare and understand only those things of which I have a clear and a distinct concept. I cannot conclude, therefore, that one who is able to do impossible things is able also to do that which is possible. I ask what conclusion is this? If any one can square a circle he can also make a circle whose radii are not equal; or if one can endue nothing with the qualities of matter he can also produce something from nothing. As I have said there is no analogy, or relation, or means of comparison between such terms. Any one who reflects upon this even a little can clearly see that this is true. Therefore I believe that something else was meant by the ingenious Descartes. Considering the second axiom given above, Descartes seemed to mean by the terms *greater and more difficult* that which was more perfect, and by the opposite terms that which was less perfect. This also certainly seems obscure. It is the same difficulty found above, and I deny here, as there, that he who has power to do the greater thing has power also at the same time to do the lesser. According to the above proposition this must be granted. Then when he says " it is greater to create or conserve substance than its attributes," we cannot understand by attributes that which is formally contained in substance and only distinguished from it by reason. For then it would be the same thing to create substance as to create attributes. For the same reason we cannot think that he meant the properties of substance. This follows necessarily from its essence and definition, much less can we understand by this, however, as he seemed to wish, the properties and attributes of some other substance; as for example, if I say that because I have the power of conserving myself, a thinking, finite substance, so I have the power of giving to myself all the perfection of infinite substance which differs by its whole essence from me. For the power or essence by which I conserve my being differs *toto genere* from the power and essence by which absolute or infinite substance conserves itself. The power and properties of infinite substance are not differentiated *per se* but only by reason; [2] so (while I may concede that I conserve myself), if I wish to think that I have the power to give to myself all the perfection of infinite substance I suppose nothing else than that I have the power to annihilate my

[2] It may be noted here that the *power* by which substance conserves itself is nothing but its essence and only differs from that in name. Which we will clearly show when in the Appendix we discuss the nature of God.

being and to create infinite substance anew. Which clearly presupposes more than that I am able to conserve the finite substance of my being. If then none of these interpretations can be given to the terms *attributes* or *properties,* nothing remains but the qualities which are eminently contained in the substance (as this or that thought which I clearly see are wanting in me). Not, however, what some other substance eminently contains; for these attributes even though wanting in me are not imperfections so far as I am considered to be a thinking being. This, then, which Descartes wished to infer from his axioms does not logically follow; namely, that if I have the power to conserve myself, I have the power also of giving to myself all the marks of perfection of the Absolute Being. This is evident from what has been said. But to avoid confusion, and to make the matter more certain, it seems best to demonstrate the following Lemmata first and give the demonstration of the seventh proposition afterward.

Lemma I.

An object of a higher degree of perfection, by virtue of this fact involves a fuller existence and a greater necessity of existence. Conversely, that which by nature involves a greater necessity of existence, is more perfect.

DEMONSTRATION.

Existence is contained in the idea or concept of every object (per Ax. 6). Let us suppose A to be an object with ten degrees of perfection. I say that this object involves more existence than if it is supposed to contain but five. For, as we cannot affirm existence of nothing (Vid. Schol. Prop. 4), as we detract from the perfection of a concept and conceive its content to approach zero as its limit, so much do we detract from its possible existence. If we conceive this degree of perfection to be infinitely diminished, even to zero, it will contain no existence, or but an absolutely impossible one. On the other hand if we increase this degree of perfection to infinity we conceive that it has the highest possible existence and so to be absolutely necessary. This was the first point to be proven. Then, as I am by no means able to separate these two (as appears from Ax. 6 and the whole of Pt. I.) it clearly follows that the other is likewise true.

Note I. *Although many things are said to exist necessarily simply because the cause producing them is given we do not now speak of such objects; but only of that necessity and possibility which follows from the mere consideration of the nature and essence of the thing itself, no reason being held as to its cause.*

Note II. *We do not here speak of beauty and other marks of perfection which men from ignorance and tradition are accustomed to esteem as such. But by perfection I understand only so much reality or being. As for example, I perceive that there is more reality in substance than in modes or qualities. And so far, I know clearly that there is necessity, and a more perfect existence in the first than in the latter two, as is evident from Axioms 4 and 6.*

COROLLARY.

Hence it follows that that which absolutely involves a necessary existence is perfect Being, or God.

Lemma II.

He who has the power of conserving himself, involves, by his nature, a necessary existence.

DEMONSTRATION.

Whoever has the power of conserving himself, has also the power of self-creation (per Ax. 10), that is, (as all will readily concede), he needs no external cause of his existence, but his own nature is sufficient cause that he should exist, either problematically or necessarily. But not problematically; for (according to what I have shown in Ax. 10) from the mere fact of existence it does not follow that an object will continue to exist; this being contrary to the hypothesis. Therefore necessarily: that is, his nature involves existence. Q. E. D.

DEMONSTRATION

Of Proposition VII.

If I had in myself the power of self-conservation I would by nature have a necessary existence (per Lemma II.), and (per Coroll. Lemm. I.); my nature would contain all the attributes of perfection. But as a thinking being I am certain that there are many imperfections in me (per Schol. Prop. 4) as that I doubt, I desire, etc. Therefore I do not have the power of self-conservation, nor can I say that I choose thus to limit my being for this is clearly opposed to Lemma I. and to what I actually experience in myself. (Per Ax. 5).

Since then it is impossible for me to exist except as I am conserved, as long as I exist, I must exist either by my own power (provided I possess such power), or by the power of another. But I exist (per Schol. Prop. 4) and yet have not the power of self-conservation as is now positively proven. Therefore I am conserved by another; but not by a being who does not possess the power of self-conservation (for the same reason that I myself do not possess this power); therefore by some being who has this power, i. e. (per Coroll. Lemm. I.) by one whose nature involves a necessary existence, and contains all perfection which I recognize as belonging to an absolutely perfect being. Therefore this perfect being, i. e., God, exists. Q. E. D.

COROLLARY.

God is able to do all that we clearly understand, just as we so understand it.

DEMONSTRATION.

This all follows from the preceding Proposition. For it was proven that God does exist from this, viz., that it is necessary for some being to exist in whom is found all the perfection we can clearly conceive. Moreover, there is in us the idea of some power so great that by it alone all things exist which are understood by me as possible, the heavens, the earth and all other things. Therefore with God's existence all of these statements are likewise proven.

PROPOSITION VIII.
Mind and body are essentially different.

DEMONSTRATION.

Whatever we clearly conceive, can be realized by God just as we so conceive it (per Coroll. of the preceding). But we clearly conceive of mind, a thinking substance (per Def. 6) apart from body, i. e. (per Def. 7), apart from extended substance (per Props. 3 and 4); and *vice versa* body apart from mind (as all will concede). Therefore, through divine power mind can exist apart from body and body apart from mind.

Substances which can exist the one apart from the other are essentially different (per Def. 10); body and mind are substances (per Defs. 5, 6, 7) which can so exist; therefore they are essentially different.

See Prop. 4 of Descartes in the end of his Response to the Second Objection; and also what is found in Pt. I. of the *Principles,* Arts. 22–29. For I consider that these things here do not give the value of the work.

PROPOSITION IX.

God is omniscient.

DEMONSTRATION.

If you deny it, then God either knows nothing or only a certain limited amount. But to understand some things and be ignorant of others implies a limitation to God's perfection, which is absurd (per Def. 8). If God understands nothing, it either indicates in God a want of intelligence and involves in Him, as in men who understand nothing, an imperfection, which is impossible with God (Ibid.), or it indicates, which is also repugnant to the idea of His being, that He understands only some things. But if intelligence is so denied to Him it is impossible for Him to create intellect (per Ax. 8). Since intellect is clearly and distinctly conceived by us, God is able to be its cause (per Coroll. Prop. 7). Therefore, it is far from being the case that He understands only some things, this being opposed to God's perfection. Therefore, God is omniscient. Q. E. D.

SCHOLIUM.

Although it must be conceded that God is incorporeal, as will be proven in Proposition 16, this does not mean only that all perfection of extension is wanting in Him, but only that the imperfections of extension must not be attributed to Him. The same is true of God's intelligence, as all, who wish to be above the rank and file of philosophers, will readily admit. This will be further explained in our Appendix, Pt. II., ch. 7.

PROPOSITION X.

Whatever perfection is found in God arises from His own being.

If you deny it, let it be supposed that there is some perfection in God which does not have its source in Himself. Either it would be in God by virtue of itself or by virtue of something apart from God. But if its cause was in itself it would have a necessary, or at least a problematical existence (per Lemma II. Prop. 7), and so far (per Coroll. Lemma I. Ibid.), have some absolute perfection and (per Def. 8) thus be God. If, therefore, we say that there is some perfection in God whose cause is itself, we affirm that it arises from God Q. E. D. But if it has arisen from some other source than God, then He is not an absolutely perfect being, which is contrary to Def. 8. Therefore whatever perfection is found in God arises from His own being. Q. E. D.

Proposition XI.

There are not many gods.

DEMONSTRATION.

If you deny this, conceive, if possible, that there are many gods, for example A and B. Then necessarily (per Prop. 9) A as well as B will be omniscient; that is, A will understand all things himself and B, and likewise B will understand himself and A. But since A and B exist necessarily (per Prop. 5), the cause of the truth and the necessity of the idea of B which A has is B himself; and likewise the cause of the truth and the necessity of the idea of A in B is in A himself. Therefore there will be some perfection in A that is not self-caused, and likewise with B. And so far A and B would not be gods. Therefore there is only one God. Q. E. D.

It should be noted here that because there is something which in itself involves a necessary existence as does God's being, He is the only being of whom this is true, as any one who reflects carefully will clearly see. I might also demonstrate this, but it is evident in all that I have shown in this Proposition.

Proposition XII.

All existing things are conserved by God's power alone.

DEMONSTRATION.

If you deny this, let it be supposed that something conserves itself. Then (per Lemma II. Prop. 7) its nature involves necessary existence. And so (per Coroll. Lemma I. Prop. 7), it would be God, and there would be more than one God, which is absurd (per Prop. supra). Therefore, nothing exists which is not conserved by God's power alone. Q. E. D.

COROLLARY I.

God is the Creator of all things.

DEMONSTRATION.

God (per the preceding) conserves all things, i. e. (per Axiom 10), he has created all things and is continually creating them.

COROLLARY II.

Objects have in themselves no essence which is the cause of God's knowledge of them.

DEMONSTRATION.

Since God's perfection is self-derived (per Prop. 10), objects can have no self-caused essence which could be the cause of God's knowledge of them. On the other hand, since God has created all things, not from other objects, but by the mere fiat of His will, (per Prop. 12 with Coroll.), and since He knows no other power beside His own (for so I define creation), it follows that before creation nothing existed, and that God is the cause of the essence of all things. Q. E. D.

It may be noted, also, that this corollary is evident from the fact that God is the cause or creator of all things (per Coroll. I.), and that the cause must contain in itself all the perfection of the effect (per Axiom 8).

COROLLARY III.

It clearly follows, therefore, that God does not, properly speaking, perceive or form precepts, for His understanding is not determined by any external object, but all things arise from Himself.

COROLLARY IV.

God's causality is prior to the essence and existence of things. This clearly follows from Corollaries I. and II. above.

PROPOSITION XIII.

God is never a deceiver, but in all things is perfectly true.

DEMONSTRATION.

We can attribute nothing to God in which we find any imperfection (per Ax. 8).[1] All deception (as is evident) or desire of deceiving, arises either from malice or fear. Fear, moreover, presupposes a limited power; malice a privation of some good. No deception, therefore, can be ascribed to God, a being omnipotent and of perfect goodness, but on the contrary, it must be agreed that He is in no way a deceiver. Q. E. D. See "Response to Second Objection," number 4.

[1] I have not put this down as an Axiom with the others, as I could not see the need of so doing. I do not use it except in demonstrating this proposition, and also, while we have not yet proved God's existence I did not wish to assume anything as true which I could not deduce from the primary truth *Ego sum* as I said in Scholium Prop. 4. Further, I have not given among the others the definitions of malice and fear for no one is ignorant of them, and I do not use them except in this place.

Proposition XIV.

Whatever we clearly and distinctly conceive, is true.

DEMONSTRATION.

The faculty we possess of discerning the true from the false (as every one finds in himself and is evident from all that has been said) has been created by God and is continually conserved by Him (per Prop. 12 and Coroll.), that is (per the above), by a Being of absolute truth and not a deceiver. Neither has He given to us (as every one knows) any power of withholding assent to what we thus clearly conceive. Wherefore if we are deceived in this, we are deceived in everything by God, and He is a deceiver, which, by the above, is absurd. Therefore, whatever we clearly and distinctly conceive is true. Q. E. D.

SCHOLIUM.

Since those things to which we are constrained to assent when we clearly and distinctly conceive them are necessarily true;-and since we have the power of withholding assent from those things which are obscure and doubtful, and not derived from certain premises (as every one understands from his own experience), it clearly follows that we are able to be on our guard lest we fall into error and are deceived (which will be made clearer as we proceed). We may, in this manner, determine in ourselves to affirm nothing which we do not clearly and distinctly conceive, or which is not deduced from certain premises.

Proposition XV.

Error is nothing positive.

DEMONSTRATION.

If error were something positive, God would be its cause, and by Him it would continually be procreated (per Prop. 12). But this is absurd (per Prop. 13). Therefore error is nothing positive. Q. E. D.

SCHOLIUM.

Since error is nothing positive in man, its cause will be merely the lack of a correct use of our freedom (per Schol. Prop. 14). We cannot say, therefore, that God is the cause of error in any sense, except as we say the absence of the sun is the cause of darkness, or as we say that God is the cause of blindness in a child having all his faculties except sight. For He has given to us understanding for a few things only. In order that it may be clearly understood how error depends entirely upon the misuse of the will, and how we may be able to avoid all error, we will call to mind the different modes of thought which we have, viz.: All modes of conception (as sensation, imagination, and pure cognition) and of volition (as desire, aversion, affirming, denying, and doubt); for all forms of thought may be referred to these two classes.

Concerning these things it may be noted: 1. That so far as mind knows objects clearly and distinctly and assents to them, it cannot be deceived (per Prop. 14); and also so far as it knows things and does not assent to them. For, although I can conceive of a winged horse, it is certain that I do not fall into error as long as I do not assent to the proposition that such a creature exists, or even while I am in doubt about it. And since to assent is nothing else than to determine the will, it follows that error depends entirely upon the use of the will.

As now more evidently appears, it should be noted: 2. That we not only have the power of assenting to those things which we clearly and distinctly conceive, but also of assenting to things conceived in some other way. For our will is determined by no limits. If one but consider for a moment it will be evident that if God should choose to give us infinite knowledge there would be no necessity for bestowing upon us a more ample power of volition in order that we might approve all that would be known under such conditions. But the power we now possess would be sufficient for assenting to infinite things. From this we learn that we give our assent to many things not deduced from certain principles. And further, it is evident that if knowledge extended as far as the power of volition, or if we could not exercise our power of volition beyond the limits of understanding, or finally, if we could but keep volition within the bounds of knowledge, we should never fall into error (per Prop. 14).

We do not have the power of attaining the first two conditions, however, for that would imply that the will was not created infinite in its nature and the understanding finite. The third condition alone remains, viz., whether we have the power of limiting the action of volition to the limits of the understanding. Since the will is free to determine itself, it follows that we have the power of restricting this faculty of assent within the limits of understanding. So, also, we can prevent ourselves from falling into error. Whence it is perfectly evident that whether or not we fall into error depends entirely upon the use we make of our free will. That our will is free is demonstrated in Art. 39, Pt. I. of the *Principles,* and in Meditation 4, and in our Appendix, the last chapter, it is also clearly shown. Although it is true that when we clearly and distinctly conceive something we cannot withhold assent, this necessity of assent does not depend upon some defect in the will, but upon its freedom and perfection. For to assent to the truth is a mark of perfection in us, as is sufficiently evident in itself; neither is the will ever more perfect or more free than when it directly determines itself. If it were possible for the mind so to do, it would give to itself this same perfection, viz., to assent necessarily to what is clearly and distinctly conceived. Wherefore it is far from being the case, that because we are not indifferent in comprehending truth, we know we are less free. On the other hand, we know that the more indifferent we are under such conditions the less freedom we possess.

It only remains to show how, in regard to man, error is privation, and in regard to God mere negation. This we will easily see if we consider first, that seeing many things beside those which we understand clearly, we are more perfect than if we did not perceive them. This is evident because, if it be supposed that we are able to conceive nothing clearly and distinctly, but only confusedly, we would have nothing more perfect than these confused concepts, neither would anything further be desired. Under such conditions, to assent to what we perceive only in a confused way, so far as the act is concerned, would be the perfect

thing to do. This will be evident to any one, if, as
above, he supposes that it is repugnant to human nature to know anything clearly or distinctly. For
though he does not attain to clearness in his knowledge, it is far better to assent to what is perceived
only confusedly, and thus to exercise his freedom,
than to remain indifferent, that is, as will be shown,
to remain in a lower degree of freedom. If we wish
to appeal to experience and utility, we will find that
daily experience teaches this same truth.

Since, therefore, all our modes of thought, considered in themselves, are perfect, the source of error is
not in the understanding. But if we consider the
different forms of volition as they differ from one
another, some are found to be more perfect than
others, for there are some that show less indifference
of will, that is, are more free. We know, also, that
as long as we give our assent to what is not clearly
and distinctly known, we are rendering ourselves the
more unfit to discern the true from the false. And
thus we do not possess the highest liberty. Therefore, to assent to what is only obscurely perceived, so
far as it is anything positive, is not in itself an imperfection or error. But it deprives us of the highest
freedom for which we are fitted. All imperfection of
error, therefore, consists in the privation of the highest form of liberty and is called *error*. It is called
privation because it deprives us of some perfection
which is consonant with our nature. It is called *error*
because, from our own fault, we are without that perfection which we might possess, did we but keep, as
far as possible, volition within the bounds of knowledge. Since error in men, therefore, is nothing else
than a privation of the perfect use of freedom, it fol-

lows that this freedom is not connected with any faculty which man has obtained from God, nor even in the operation of a faculty so far as it depends upon God. Nor can we say that He has deprived us of a more perfect knowledge with which, in order that we should not fall into error, He might have endowed us. For no one has a right to demand anything of God, nor has an object any properties except those which God of His own free will has given it. Nothing existed before the will of God, nor, as we will clearly show in chaps. 7 and 8 of our Appendix, can anything be conceived to have existed. God, therefore, has no more deprived us of a fuller understanding, or of the faculty of a more perfect knowledge, than He has deprived the circle of the properties of the globe or its periphery of the properties of the sphere.

Since, then, nothing in our powers, however considered, reveals any imperfection in God, it clearly follows that error in man is nothing but privation; but relative to God as its cause, it is not privation, but negation.

PROPOSITION XVI.

God is incorporeal.

DEMONSTRATION.

Matter is the immediate subject of motion (per Def. 7); therefore, if God is corporeal, He may be divided into parts. This, however, since it involves an imperfection, it is absurd to affirm.

ANOTHER PROOF.

If God were corporeal, He might be divided into parts (per Def. 7). Now, either each part would be able to subsist *per se* or it would not. If the former, each part would be similar to other things erected by God and constantly conserved by His power (per Prop. 10 and Ax. 11). These parts would then pertain no more to the nature of God than do other created objects, as is evident from Prop. 5. But if each part exists by its own power, they would each involve a necessary existence (per Lemma II. Prop. 7), and consequently would be a perfect being (per Coroll. Lemma II. Prop. 7). But this also is absurd (per Prop. II.). Therefore God is incorporeal. Q. E. D.

PROPOSITION XVII.

God is simple being (ens simplissimum).

DEMONSTRATION.

If God were composite in His nature, these parts, as all will readily concede, should be prior, even down to the most insignificant one, to the nature of God, which is absurd (per Coroll. 4, Prop. 12). Therefore God is simple being. Q. E. D.

COROLLARY.

Hence it follows that God's understanding, His volition, His decrees and His power are only distinctions of reason.

Proposition XVIII.

God is unchangeable.

DEMONSTRATION.

If God were changeable, He would not change in part, but His whole essence would change (per Prop. 7). But God's essence is necessarily what it is (per Props. 5, 6 and 7); therefore God is unchangeable. Q. E. D.

Proposition XIX.

God is eternal.

DEMONSTRATION.

God is a perfect being (Def. 8), and therefore necessarily exists. If we attribute only a limited existence to Him these limits must be known, if not by us, by God Himself (per Prop. 9), who is omniscient. But then God who is omniscient (per Def. 8), would know no existence beyond these limits, which is absurd (per Prop. 5). Therefore God does not have a limited but an infinite existence, which we call eternity. (*Vid. Chap. I., Part II., of our Appendix.*) God, therefore, is eternal. Q. E. D.

Proposition XX.

God has preordained everything from eternity.

DEMONSTRATION.

Since God is eternal (per Prop. 19), His understanding is eternal because it pertains to His eternal

essence (per Coroll. Prop. 7). Hence His understanding, and His will, and His decrees are one (Ibid.)
Therefore when we say God knows all things from
eternity, we say also that He has willed, and decreed
them from eternity. Q. E. D.

COROLLARY.

From this proposition it follows that God is unchangeable in all His works.

PROPOSITION XXI.

*Extended substance has three dimensions, length,
breadth and depth. We are united with each of these
three.*

DEMONSTRATION.

Extended substance, so far as we clearly understand
it, does not pertain to the nature of God (per Prop.
10). It can, however, be created by God (per Coroll.
Prop. 7, and per Prop. 8). Then we clearly and distinctly perceive (as every thinking person knows) that
extended substance produces in us titulations or pain
and other similar sensations or ideas, at times even
contrary to our desires. If we attempt to find some
other cause of our sensations, as for example God or
an angel, we immediately destroy the clear concept
which we had before. Therefore (Vid. demonstration
Prop. 14 and Schol. Prop. 15), as long as we properly
attend to our perceptions and do not admit what is not
clearly and distinctly known, we lose our indifference
and are led to admit that extended substance alone is
the cause of our sensations. So, also, we will see and
admit that extended things were created and exist by

God's power. In this we are clearly not deceived
(per Prop. 14 with Schol.). Therefore it is truly
affirmed that extended substance has length, and
breadth, and depth, which was the first point.

And further, as I have already proven, we observe
great differences between our various sensations, as
for example, when I say I perceive or see a tree; or
when I say I am thirsty, or suffer, etc. It is evident
that I cannot see or understand the reasons for these
differences, unless I know that as a being, I am united
to certain portions of matter and not to others. When
I understand this clearly, and there is no other way
to know it, it is evident that I am united to a certain
part of matter. This was the second point, and it is
now proven. Q. E. D.

Note.— *Unless the reader considers himself merely
as a thinking being and free from his body, and lays
aside as prejudices all the reasons he has heretofore
held as proving the existence of the body, he will attempt in vain to understand this demonstration.*

The Principles of Philosophy Demonstrated by the Method of Geometry.

PART II.

A POSTULATE.

It is only asked here that each one attend as accurately as possible to his concepts in order to be able to distinguish the clear from the obscure.

DEFINITIONS.

I. *Extension* is that which consists of three dimensions. We do not understand by the term the act of extending or anything else distinct from quantity.

II. By *substance* we understand that which depends only upon the concurrence of God for its existence.

III. An *Atom* as a part of matter, by nature is indivisible.

IV. That is *indefinite*, the limits of which, if it has any, cannot be investigated by the human mind.

V. A *vacuum* is extension without corporeal substance.

VI. *Space* is distinguished from *extension* only by the reason; in reality they are one and the same thing. See Art. 10, Pt. II. of the *Principles*.

VII. That which we understand to be divisible, is divisible, at least potentially.

VIII. *Local motion* is the transference of a particle of matter or of a body from the vicinity of other contiguous bodies considered as in a state of rest, to the vicinity of others.

This definition Descartes used to explain local motion. In order to understand this rightly it should be noted:

1. That by a particle of matter he understood all that which is transferred at the same time, although it may itself be composed of many parts.

2. That to avoid confusion in this definition he spoke only of that which is always in moving bodies, viz., transference, lest, as has often happened, this be confused with the force or action which transfers them. This force or action, it is generally believed, is required only for motion and not for rest, which belief is plainly wrong. For, as is self-evident, the same force is required to give to a body at rest a certain velocity as is required to bring the same body with that given velocity to rest. This is proved also by experience. Almost the same force is used in starting a ship at rest in quiet water as in suddenly stopping it when in motion. Plainly this force would be the same except that we are assisted in retarding the motion of the ship by the weight and viscosity of the retarding water.

3. That, he says, the transference is made from the vicinity of contiguous bodies to the vicinity of others and not from one place to another. For place (as he himself explained Art. 13, Pt. 2) is not something in the object, but it depends upon our thought, so much so that the same body may be said at the same time to change its place and not to change it; but not at the same time to be transferred from the vicinity of

contiguous bodies and not to be transferred. For only one body at the same moment of time can be contiguous to the same moving body.

4. That he did not say absolutely that a transference was made from the vicinity of contiguous bodies, but only so far as they were considered to be at rest.

 For in order that the body A be transferred from the body B at rest, the same force is required whether in this direction or in that. This is evident from the example of a boat aground or on the sand in shallow water. For in order that the boat may be moved an equal force must be exerted against the boat and against the ground. Therefore the force by which bodies are moved is expended equally on the moving body and on the one at rest. The action and the reaction are equal. If the boat is moved from the sand, the sand is likewise moved from the boat. If, of bodies which are mutually separated, the one to this place, the other to that, we attribute equal motion, then regard one of them as at rest, it is because the same action is in one as in the other. Then also even to bodies which are regarded by all as at rest, e. g., the sand from which the boat is separated, we are compelled to attribute to this a motion equal to the motion of the boat; for, as we have shown, the same action is required in the one part as in the other, and the transposition is reciprocal. But this is too much at variance with the common way of speaking. In truth, although, those bodies from which others are separated are regarded as at rest and are also said to be so, nevertheless we affirm that everything in the moving body on account of which it is said to be moving is also in the body at rest.

5. Finally, from the definition it is evident that every body has for itself its own one proper motion, since only in regard to contiguous quiet bodies is it said to recede. Nevertheless, if a moving body is a part of other bodies having other motions, we clearly see that it is also able to participate in these as well. But because so many things can not easily be understood, nor will all recognize this, it will suffice to consider that alone which is peculiar to each body. See Art. 31, Pt. 2, *Principles.*

IX. By a *circle of moving bodies* we understand such an arrangement that when one is impelled by the impulse of another the last immediately touches the first one of the series; although the line described by the motion of these bodies may plainly be contorted.

AXIOMS.

_. To non-being there are no properties.

II. Whatever can be detracted from an object, without destroying the completeness of that object, does not constitute its essence; that which, when taken away, destroys the object does constitute its essence.

III. As to hardness sense indicates nothing else, nor do we clearly and distinctly know more than that the parts of hard bodies resist the motion of our hands.

IV. Whether two bodies are mutually approaching one another, or whether receding, they occupy the same amount of space.

V. A particle of matter, whether it gives way to or resists another, does not lose its character.

VI. Motion, rest, form, and similar ideas cannot be conceived without the concept of extension.

VII. Beside the sensible qualities of bodies, nothing remains except extension and its affects as given in Part I. of the *Principles*.

VIII. One space or portion of extension is no greater than another.

IX. All extension can be divided, at least, in thought. Concerning the truth of this axiom no one can doubt who has learned even the elements of mathematics. For the space between a given circle and its tangent can always be divided by an infinite number of greater circles. Which is also true as regards the asymptote of the hyperbole.

X. No ends of extension or space can be conceived except as another space is conceived to immediately follow such limits.

XI. If matter were manifold and one part did not immediately touch the other, each part would necessarily be comprehended under limits beyond which no matter is given.

XII. A very minute body easily recedes before the motion of our hands.

XIII. One space does not penetrate another, nor is the one greater than the other.

XIV. If the tube A is of equal length with C, but C is twice as large as A, then if some liquid flows through A with double the velocity of that which passes through C, in the same time an equal amount will have passed through each. And if, in an equal time, an equal quantity has passed through each, the velocity through A will be double that of C.

XV. Things which agree in a third part agree in

the whole. And things which are each double a third part are equal to one another.

XVI. Matter which is moved in different ways has at least as many divided parts as there were degrees of swiftness observed at any given time.

XVII. A straight line is the shortest distance between two points.

XVIII. A body A moving from C toward B, if repelled by a contrary impulse, will move along the same line toward C.

XIX. Bodies having motions in opposite directions, when they come in contact, undergo some change.

XX. Variation in any object proceeds from a stronger force.

XXI. If when body 1 is moved toward body 2 and impels it, and body 8 from this impulse is moved toward 1, bodies 1, 2, 3, etc., cannot be in a straight line. But all of them from 1 to 8 compose a complete circle (Vid. Def. 9).

LEMMA I.

Where there is extension or space, there from necessity substance also exists.

DEMONSTRATION.

Extension or space (per Ax. 1) cannot be pure nothing; therefore it is an attribute which must be attributed to something. But not to God (per Prop. 16, Part I.); therefore to some object which needs only God's concurrence for its existence (per Prop. 12, Part I.), that is (per Def. 2), to substance. Q. E. D.

LEMMA II.

We clearly and distinctly conceive of rarefaction and condensation. We would not concede, however, that a body occupies more space under rarefaction than under condensation.

DEMONSTRATION.

We can have a clear and a distinct concept of these because we can conceive that the parts of a body mutually recede, or mutually approach one another. Therefore (per Ax. 4), they will not occupy more or less space. If the parts of some body, for example a sponge, are compressed the bodies between the parts will be occupied. What we can thus clearly perceive occupy less space than before (per Ax. 4). And if, again, the body expands and the pores are filled by some body, there is a rarefaction, but no more space will be occupied. What we can thus clearly perceive by the senses in the case of the sponge, we can conceive by the understanding to be true with all bodies, although the pores of these cannot be perceived by our senses. Therefore, rarefaction and condensation are clearly conceived, etc. Q. E. D.

It seemed best to give this at this place in order to overcome these prejudices concerning space, rarefaction, etc., and in order that the mind may be ready to understand what follows.

PROPOSITION I.

Although hardness, weight, and the other sensible qualities of a body be removed, the whole nature of that body will nevertheless remain.

DEMONSTRATION.

In the hardness of this stone, for example, sense indicates nothing to us, nor can we clearly and distinctly conceive anything, except that its parts resist the movements of our hands (per Ax. 3). Therefore (per Prop. 14, Part I.), hardness is nothing but this. If that body were pulverized into very small particles, these parts would easily give way (per Ax. 12); nevertheless, they do not lose the nature of the body (per Ax. 5). Q. E. D.

In regard to weight and to other sensible qualities, the same demonstration is valid.

PROPOSITION II.

The nature of body or matter (corporis sive materiæ) *consists in extension alone.*

DEMONSTRATION.

The nature of body is not destroyed by the loss of sensible qualities (per Prop. 1 above); therefore these do not constitute its essence (per Ax. 2). Nothing remains except extension and its affects (per Ax. 7). Therefore, if extension is destroyed, nothing will remain which pertains to the nature of body, but it is destroyed; therefore (per Ax. 2), the nature of body consists in extension alone. Q. E. D.

COROLLARY.

Space and Body are the same.

DEMONSTRATION.

Body and extension are the same (per the preceding); space and extension are the same thing (per Def. 6); therefore (per Ax. 15), space and body are the same. Q. E. D.

SCHOLIUM.

Although we have said [1] that God is omnipresent we do not believe that God is extension, that is, (per the preceding) body. His omnipotence pertains only to his power and his concurrence by which all things are conserved. So far, therefore, His omnipresence refers no more to extension or body than to angels or to the human mind. It should be noted, too, that when we say His power is everywhere we do not exclude His essence: for where His power is, there His essence is also (Coroll. Prop. 17, Part I.). We would exclude corporeality, that is, God is not everywhere in some corporeal power, but in divine essence, which is common in the preservation of extension and in thinking being (Prop. 17, Part I.). These He would not be able to perfectly conserve if His power or essence were corporeal.

PROPOSITION III.

It is a contradiction to say that a vacuum exists.

DEMONSTRATION.

By a vacuum is meant extension without corporeal substance (per Def. 5), that is (per Prop. 2), body without body, which is absurd.

[1] Vid. Appendix, Pt. II., Chaps. III. and IX.

For a fuller explanation of this proposition, and to correct the prejudices men have concerning a vacuum, Articles 17 and 18, Part II. of the "Principles," should be read. In these it is noted more especially that bodies between which nothing intervenes necessarily touch one another, and, also, that there are no properties to non-being.

PROPOSITION IV.

One particle of a body occupies at one time no more space than another; conversely, the same space at a given time will contain no more of one body than of another.

DEMONSTRATION.

Space and body are the same thing (per Coroll. Prop. 2): therefore when we say that one portion of space is no larger than another (per Ax. 13) we affirm that a body cannot occupy more space in one place than in another, which was the first point to be proved.

Further, from the fact that space does not differ from body, it follows, that when we say that a body cannot occupy more space in one place than in another, we likewise affirm that the same space cannot contain more of one body than another. Q. E. D.

COROLLARY.

Bodies which occupy an equal amount of space, as for example some gold and some brass, have an equal amount of matter or of corporeal substance.

DEMONSTRATION.

Corporeal substance does not consist in hardness, e. g. of gold, nor in softness, e. g. of brass, nor in any sensible quality (per Prop. 1, above), but in extension alone (per Prop. 2 above). Moreover, since by hypothesis there is an equal amount of space or (per Def. 6) of extension in the one as in the other, there is a like amount of corporeal substance. Q. E. D.

PROPOSITION V

There are no Atoms.

DEMONSTRATION.

By their nature atoms are indivisible parts of matter (per Def. 3). But since the nature of matter consists in extension (per Prop. 2 above), which by nature is divisible, however small the part (per Ax. 9 and Def. 7), it follows that any part of matter, however small, is divisible. That is, there are no atoms or indivisible parts of matter. Q. E. D.

SCHOLIUM.

The question of atoms has always been a great and an intricate one. Some affirm that atoms must exist because one infinity cannot be greater than another; and if two bodies, A and one double the size of A, are divisible to infinity by the power of God, who understands their infinite parts in one intuition, they can actually be so divided. Therefore, as it is said, since one infinity is no greater than another, one part of A will be equal to one double its size, which is

absurd. Then they ask also, whether a part divided
half way to infinity would still be infinite, and
whether it would be equal or unequal, and other
things of this kind. To this question Descartes replied that we ought not to reject what we properly
understand on account of other things which surpass
our understanding, and which consequently cannot
adequately be conceived. Infinity and its properties
are beyond the power of the human intellect, which
is by nature finite. It would, then, be improper to
reject as false what we clearly and distinctly conceive, or to doubt this because we do not understand
the infinite. Hence, Descartes held that those things
which have no limits, such as the extension of the
world or the divisibility of a part of matter, should
be called *indefinite*. See Art. 26, Part I. *Principles.*

Proposition VI.

*Matter is indefinitely extended, and is the same
throughout the heavens and the earth.*

DEMONSTRATION.

Point I. No limit to extension or matter can be
conceived (per Prop. 2 above) except as we conceive
of another space, that is (per Def. 6), extension or
matter immediately following this (per Ax. 10), and
so on indefinitely; which was the first point to be
proved.

Point II. The essence of matter consists in extension (per Prop. 2 above), and this is indefinite
(per Point I.). That is (per Def. 4), it cannot be
conceived to be bounded by any limits; therefore
(per Ax. 11), it is not manifold in its nature but every-

where one and the same; which was the second point
to be proved.

We have already discussed the nature and essence
of matter. In the last Proposition to Part I. we
showed that matter created by God's power exists, as
it is conceived by us, and from Proposition 12 of the
same part it follows that it is conserved by the same
power that created it. Also, in the last Proposition to
Part I. we showed that so far as we are thinking
beings, we are united to some part of matter. Hence,
we are certain that all the changes in matter are real,
which we, by the contemplation of matter, perceive
as possible. As, for example, that matter is divisible
or capable of motion, that there may be a transference of some parts of matter from one place to another, which, indeed, we clearly and distinctly know,
provided we understand that other parts take the place
of those which are moved. This division and motion
is conceived by us in infinite modes, hence an infinite
variation of matter is conceived as possible. I say that
these things are clearly and distinctly conceived by us
(as was clearly explained in Part I. of the *Principles*)
so long as they are regarded as modes of extension, and
not as objects apart from extension. And although
some philosophers conceive of many forms of motion,
we only admit that there is local motion. For it is evident to us, who admit only what is clearly and distinctly
perceived, that extension is capable only of local motion, neither can any other form be imagined.

Zeno, indeed, it is said, for various reasons denied
that there was motion in space (*motum localum*),
which assertion the cynic Diogenes refuted in a char-

acteristic way, namely, by walking about in the school
where Zeno was teaching, and thus disturbing his
pupils. When he was asked by a certain listener
to stop his walking he began to find fault with him
by saying: "Why do you thus dare to refute the
teaching of your master?" But lest any one, perchance, deceived by this argument of Zeno, should
think that the senses show anything to us, as for example motion, which is at variance with the understanding, so that the mind is deceived about those
things, which, by the help of the intellect are perceived
clearly and distinctly, I shall give his principal reasons, and show that these are only supported by false
prejudices; namely, because he had no true concept of
matter.

In the first place it is said that he argued that if
there is motion in space, the motion of a body moving
in a circle with the greatest possible speed does not
differ from a body at rest; and this is absurd, therefore, that also. Consequently, he affirmed this.
That body is at rest, all of whose parts constantly remain in the same place; but all the parts of a body
moving in a circle with the greatest possible velocity
constantly remain in the same place. Therefore, etc.,

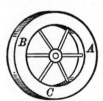

This, it is said, he explained by the
example of a wheel, for example
A, B, C. Which, if it moves with
a certain velocity about its center,
the point A will move more rapidly
through the points B and C than
if it rotated more slowly. Let it be
supposed for example, that when moving slowly for an
hour, the point A occupies the same point as when it
began. If it moves with double this velocity, in a half-

hour it will occupy the same point, and if with a velocity four times as great, then in a quarter of an hour.
If, now, we conceive that the velocity is increased to infinity, and the time to be diminished even to a moment, then the point A, moving with this infinite
velocity every moment, or continually, will be in the
place from which it began to move. So far it will
always remain in the same place. And this, which is
true of the point A, is also true of every other point
of the wheel. Therefore, all points of a body moving
with the highest velocity remain in the same place.

Indeed, as I would reply, it should be noted that this
is more an argument against *infinite motion* than
against motion itself. We shall not, however, inquire
whether Zeno argued rightly, but rather would detect
those prejudices on which the whole argument rests
so far as he thought this to annul the idea of motion.
In the first place it is supposed that a body may be
conceived to be moving so fast that a greater velocity
is impossible. Then, again, it is supposed that time
is composed of moments, as some think that quantity
is made up of indivisible points. Both suppositions
are false. For we are not able to conceive of a motion
than which there can be no greater. It is contrary to
reason to think there is a motion, however small the
line it describes, so rapid that no more rapid one can
be given. The same thing holds true in regard to
slowness. For it implies that we can conceive of a
motion so slow that a slower one can not be given.
Concerning *time* also, which is a measure of motion,
we affirm that the same thing is true, and that it is
contrary to reason to think of a time so short that no
shorter can be given. All of which, as we will prove,
follows from the words of Zeno. Let it be supposed,

therefore, as he said, that the wheel A, B, C, rotates with such speed that the point A at all moments is in the point A from which it moves. I say that I can clearly conceive that this swiftness is indefinitely increased and these moments of time to be diminished in inverse ratio. For let it be supposed that while the wheel A, B, C, is rotating, another wheel, D, E, F, (which I suppose half as large as the other), is made to rotate by the chord H. Since the wheel D, E, F is only half the size of A, B, C, it is evident that the first one will rotate twice as fast as the latter. Then if the wheel A, B, C is supposed to have the motion of D, E, F, the movement of D, E, F will be

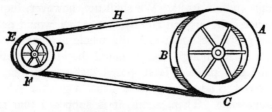

four times the original motion of A, B, C. And if we suppose this motion of D, E, F to be given to A, B, C, the motion of D, E, F will be eight times the motion of our original wheel. And so on to infinity. This is perfectly evident from the very concept of matter. For as we have proven the essence of matter consists in extension or in space always divisible. There is no motion except in space. We showed also that the same part of matter cannot occupy two points of space at the same time. This would be equal to saying that one part of matter is equal to another part twice its size. Therefore, if a particle of matter is moved it is moved through some space. This space, and the time that serves to measure this as well, how-

ever small they be conceived to be, will always be
divisible. Q. E. D.

We turn now to another argument of the same
nature. If a body is moved, does it move in the place
in which it is, or in some other? It does not move
in the place where it is, for if it is any where it is
necessarily at rest. Neither can it move in a place
where it is not. Therefore, a body does not move.
This argument is plainly similar to the first, for it
also supposes that there is a time given than which
there can be no smaller. For if you reply that a body
does not move *in* the place it is, but *from* that place to
another, he will ask whether it does not also move
through the intervening places. We reply by making a distinction — if through the term *was* we understand *to be at rest* then we deny that the body was
at any of the places through which it moved: but if by
was existence is meant, then we say that it necessarily
existed in that point although it was moving. But he
would also ask whether it existed any where while
it was moving. We reply, if he meant to ask whether
the body remained in any one place, that it did not;
but if he wished to ask whether it changed its position,
we reply that it has, through all the points in the given
distance. Then he would inquire whether it could
occupy, and move from a point at the same moment
of time. To this we reply by making another distinction. If by a moment of time he understands a
duration so short that no shorter is conceivable, as
was shown above, he asks a question that is not intelligible, and hence unworthy of reply.

But if he take time in the true sense explained
above, however small the duration assigned, it will
never be so small that a body may not both occupy it

and be moving at the same time. This is evident to any one who considers the matter. For it is evident, as we said above, that he supposes a time given than which no smaller is possible. Hence, he proves nothing.

Beside these two there is another argument of Zeno which, together with its refutation, is given in Descartes (Vol. I. "Epis.," last letter but one).

I wish here to remind the reader that my argument is opposed to the reasonings of Zeno; and that as far as he argued from reason not from sense, he followed the argument of Diogenes. Nor does sense ever give any truth to the inquirer, except the mere phenomena of Nature, whose causes he is impelled to investigate; never does it show anything to be false which the understanding clearly comprehends as true. So we believe, and so far this is our Method:—to demonstrate the things we set forth, by reasons clearly and distinctly perceived by the understanding; holding to these, whatever the senses may give that seems contrary to this; which, as we have said, can only determine the understanding as it inquires about this or that, but cannot prove the falsity of anything which is clearly and distinctly perceived.

PROPOSITION VII.

No body moves to the place of another, except as that other moves into the position of some other.

DEMONSTRATION.[1]

If you deny this, let it be supposed, if possible, that a body A take the position of a body B, and is equal

[1] Vid. Fig. Prop. seq.

to it, and also that B does not recede from its place. Then the space which before only contained B (by hypothesis) will contain A and B, and so twice as much corporeal substance as it before contained. Which (per Prop. 4 of this Part) is absurd. Therefore, no body can take the place of another, etc. Q. E. D.

PROPOSITION VIII.

When some body takes the place of another, at the same moment the place left by the one is occupied by another which is immediately contiguous to it.

DEMONSTRATION.

If the body B moves toward D, either the bodies A and C mutually approach and touch one another, or they do not. If they mutually approach and are contiguous the question is conceded. If they do not approach one another, but the space left by B lies

between them, then (per Coroll. Prop. 2 supra, and Coroll. Prop. 4) some body equal to B lies between. But (per hypothesis) not B: therefore, some other body, which at the same moment takes its place. But since it is at the same moment it is no other than the one immediately contiguous (per Schol., Prop. 6). There it was shown that there can not be motion from one place to another which does not require a duration than which a shorter may always be conceived. Hence, it follows that the space of the body B cannot be occupied at the same moment by a body which must be moved from some other position. Therefore, only the body immediately contiguous to B can occupy this space at the given moment. Q. E. D

SCHOLIUM.

Since the parts of matter are really distinct from one another (per Art. 61, Part I. *Principles*), one part can exist apart from the other (per Coroll. Prop. 7, Part I.) and they are not dependent upon one another. Therefore, all the fancies about sympathy and antipathy should be rejected as false. And further, since the cause of an effect must be positive (per Ax. 8, Part I.) we can not say that the cause of motion is a vacuum, but that it is due to the impulse of some other body.

COROLLARY.

In all motion the whole circle of bodies is moved.

DEMONSTRATION

At the moment when body 1 takes the place of body 2, this one must move into place of body 3, etc. (per Prop. 7). Then at the moment when 1 is occupying

the place of 2, the place it formerly held must (per Prop. 8) be filled by some other body, for example by 8, or some other body contiguous to 1. But since this can only come from the impulse of another body (per Schol. sup.) which is here supposed to be 1, the series cannot lie in a straight line (per Ax. 21) but (per Def. 9) describes a complete circle. Q. E. D.

Proposition IX.

If a circular canal, A, B, C, is filled with water or with some other fluid, and at A the canal is four times as broad as at B, when the water (or liquid) at A begins to move toward B, the water at B will move four times as fast as the water at A.

DEMONSTRATION.

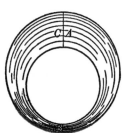

When the water at A moves toward B, the water at C, which is contiguous to A, takes its place (per Prop. 8); then from B an equal quantity must replace that at C. (per eandem). Therefore (per Ax. 14), it will move four times as fast. Q. E. D.

What we have just said concerning circular channels is also true of all unequal spaces through which water is forced. For the proof would be the same in all such cases.

Lemma.

If two semicircles are described from the same center, as for example A and B, the distance between them is equal at all points. But if they are described

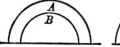

from different centers as are C and D. the distance between them is unequal at all points. This is evident from the definition of the circle.

PROPOSITION X.

A fluid body moving through the channel A, B, C, changes its velocity by indefinite degrees.

DEMONSTRATION.

(Vid. Figure to Prop. IX). The space between A and B is unequal at all points (per Lemm. sup.) ; therefore (per Prop. 9) the velocity with which a fluid moves through this channel is everywhere unequal. And since we can conceive that the space between A and B to be indefinitely divided (per Prop. 5), the inequalities also will be indefinitely changing and also (per Prop. 9) the motion by indefinite degrees. Q. E. D.

PROPOSITION XI.

In the matter which passes through the channel A, B, C, there is a division into indefinitely small parts.

DEMONSTRATION.

(Vid. Fig. Prop. 9). The matter flowing through A, B, C, has a motion changing by indefinite degrees (per Prop. 10) ; therefore (per Ax. 16) its parts must be indefinitely divided Q. E. D. See also Articles 34 and 35, Part II. " Principles."

SCHOLIUM.

We have already spoken of the nature of motion. It behooves us here to inquire into its cause, which is twofold: the primary or general cause, which is the cause of all the motion in the world, and then more specifically, how does it happen that particular objects which have no motion, acquire it. Regarding the general cause of motion it is clear, since we ought not to admit anything except what is clearly and distinctly perceived (per Prop. 14, Pt. I. and Schol. Prop. 17, Pt. II.), and since we understand no other cause except God (the creator of matter), that no other general cause of motion can be admitted except God. And what we have said of motion is also true of rest.

PROPOSITION XII.

God is the principal cause of motion.

DEMONSTRATION.

See the Scholium just given.

PROPOSITION XIII.

God by his power conserves the same quantity of motion and rest which he once gave to matter.

DEMONSTRATION.

Since God is the cause of motion and of rest (per Prop. 12), he conserves these by the same power by which he also created them (per Ax. 10 Pt. I.), and indeed with the same amount of power (per Coroll. Prop. 20, Pt. I.) Q. E. D.

SCHOLIUM.

I. Although, in Theology, it is said that God does many things because He is pleased to do so, and to show His power to man, since these acts are known only through divine revelation, they should not be admitted into the body of philosophical truth where reason is the criterion of truth, lest Theology and Philosophy become confused.

II. Although motion is nothing but a mode of a moving body, nevertheless, it has a certain definite quantity. How this is possible will appear below. See Art. 36, Pt. II. of the " Principles."

PROPOSITION XIV.

Every object, so far as it is simple and individual considered in itself alone, has a certain unchanging quantity.

To many this proposition is, as it were, an axiom; nevertheless we will give a demonstration of its truth.

DEMONSTRATION.

Since an object can exist in a certain state only by the concurrence of God (per Prop. 12, Pt. I.), and since God is unchanging in all His works (per Coroll. Prop. 20, Pt. I.), if we consider no external causes (i. e., particular ones) but consider the object in itself, it must be admitted that its quantity always remains the same. Q. E. D.

COROLLARY.

A body when once in motion will continue to move unless hindered by some external forces.

DEMONSTRATION.

This is evident from the preceding Proposition. Nevertheless for correcting certain prejudices concerning motion read Articles 37 and 38, Part II. " Principles."

Proposition XV.

Every moving body, in itself, tends to move in a straight line not in a curved one. This proposition might be given as an axiom but I will demonstrate it from the preceding ones.

DEMONSTRATION.

Motion since it has God alone as its cause (per Prop. 12, Pt. II.) has in itself no power of existence (per Ax. 10, Pt. I.), but is, as it were, procreated every single moment by God (per that which was demonstrated with the axiom just cited). Therefore, as long as we consider the mere nature of motion we cannot attribute to it, as pertaining to its nature, a duration so great that a greater may not be conceived. But if it is said that it pertains to the nature of a moving body to move in a curved line, a longer duration is attributed to the nature of motion than if it is supposed to be the nature of motion to move in a straight line (per Ax. 8). Since (as we have already demonstrated) we cannot assign such a duration to the nature of motion, we cannot suppose that it is in the nature of a moving body to move in a curved line but it must tend to move in a straight line. Q. E. D.

SCHOLIUM.

To many, perhaps, this demonstration will not seem to prove that a moving body tends to describe a straight line rather than a curved one, for no straight line can be assigned so small that there may not be a smaller either curved or straight, neither is there any curved line so small that there may not also be another curved one still smaller. Although I have considered these objections I do not consider them to be valid. For we have based our conclusion upon the universal essence of these lines, not upon the quantity of each or accidental differences. But that I may not in this demonstration render obscure what is clear, I refer the reader to the definition of motion, which affirms nothing of motion except a transference of one part of matter from one vicinity to the position of others, etc. This is true so far as we conceive of a simple transference, that is, that this is made in a straight line. So far as we go beyond this we assign something to motion which is not in the definition and so far does not pertain to its nature.

COROLLARY.

From this it follows that every body moving in a curved line is continually deflected from the line which it tends to follow. This is done by some external force (per Prop. 14, Pt. II.).

PROPOSITION XVI.

Every body moving in a circular orbit, as for example a stone in a sling, tends constantly to move off at a tangent.

DEMONSTRATION.

A body moving in a circumference is continuously restrained by some external force from moving in a straight line (per Coroll., Prop. XV. Pt. II.). When this ceases to act the body at once moves off in a straight line (per Prop. 15). I say also, that a body describing a circle continually tends to move off at a tangent. For, if you deny it let it be supposed that

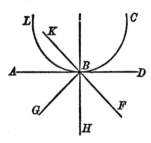

the stone, for example, in the sling at B, does not tend to follow the line BD, but some other line, either within or without the circle, for example, BF. Or the line BG (which I understand intersects the line BH, drawn from the center of the circle at B and makes with it an angle equal to the angle FBH), if it is supposed that the sling is moving from C toward B. But if the stone moving from L to B at B, tends to move in the line BF, then (per Axiom 18) when the sling moves from C toward B, it should tend to move toward K, not toward G, which is contrary to the hypothesis. And since there is no line that can be drawn through the point B except the tangent AD, which keeps the angles DBH, and ABH equal, there is no line except this tangent able to fulfil the hypothesis, when the sling is moving either from L to B or from C to B. Therefore no other line except the tangent can be drawn on which the body tends to move. Q. E. D.

ANOTHER DEMONSTRATION.[1]

In place of a circle let the hexagon A, B, H, be inscribed in a circle and a body C be at rest on one side AB. Then let the ruler DBE (one end fixed at D and the other end free) be moved about the center D, continually intersecting the line AB. It is evident that if the ruler DBE, while it is thus conceived

[1] The letter A at the intersection of the circle and the hexagon between B and G is omitted in the Latin text.

to move meet some body at C, when the ruler intersects the line AB at a right angle it will tend to
move C in the line FBAG
toward G, that is, along the
line AB produced indefinitely. Indeed, since we can consider the number of sides of
the polygon to be increased *ad
libitum,* it can be affirmed of
any figure whatever that can
be inscribed in a circle that
when a body C at rest on one
of its sides, is impelled by a ruler fixed at the center,
when the angle found by the side of the polygon and
the ruler is a right angle, the body will tend to move
in the line of that side indefinitely produced.

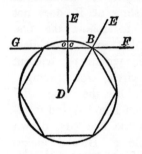

Let us conceive instead of the hexagon a polygon
of an infinite number of sides (that is, the circle according to the definition of Archimedes); then it is
clear that wherever the ruler shall come in contact
with the body C, it would always meet it at a right
angle. Hence it would never come in contact with C,
without C at the same time tending to move in the
line of that side produced. Any side whatever when
produced will lie wholly outside the figure, and this
side indefinitely produced is the tangent of one side
of the figure of an infinite number of sides, that is, of
a circle. Therefore if we think of sling moving in a
circle in place of the ruler the stone will constantly
tend to move in a tangent to that circle. Q. E. D.

*It should be noted that this demonstration can be ap-
plied to any curved figure.*

Proposition XVII.

Every body moving in a circle tends to move from the center of the circle it describes.

DEMONSTRATION.

As long as a body is moving in a circular path, so long is it held in its course by some external force; this force being removed it at once begins to move

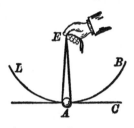

off at a tangent (per the above) all of whose points except that which touches the circle fall outside of the circle (per Prop. 16, Lib. 3, Elements), and so are further removed from the center of its path. Therefore, when the stone in the sling EA, is at the point A it will tend to move along a straight line whose points are all further from the center E than those of the circumference LAB. This is to do nothing else than to recede from the circle which it is describing. Q. E. D.

Proposition XVIII.

If some body A is moved against another body B at rest, and B acquires no motion from the impact, then A has lost none of its motion but retains all it had before.

DEMONSTRATION.

  If you deny it, let it be supposed that A has lost some of its motion but has not transferred it to another body as, for example, B. If this happens there will be less motion in Nature than before which is absurd (per

Prop. 13). The demonstration in respect to the *rest* in B is the same.[1] Therefore if no motion is transferred B will be in the same state of rest and A will retain the same amount of motion. Q. E. D.

PROPOSITION XIX.

Motion, considered in itself, by its own determination moves in a given direction; nor is there any need for a moment of rest before it can change its direction or be repelled.

DEMONSTRATION.

Let it be supposed as in the preceding proposition that a body A is moved directly against B and impeded by B but that B is not moved. Therefore (by the above) A will retain all of its motion, nor does it remain at rest even for a moment. Nevertheless when it moves it does not move in the same direction as before, for it is supposed to be impeded by the body B. Therefore its motion remaining entire and its prior determination being lost it will move in some other direction (per what was said in Chap. 2, Diopt.); and so far (per Ax. 2) determination does not pertain to the essence of motion, nor is a moving body when repelled at rest at any time. Q. E. D

COROLLARY.

Hence it follows that motion is not the opposite of motion.

---

[1] Spinoza throughout this work attributes quantity to *rest* or quietude just as he does to motion; a body may have a certain amount of rest as well as a certain amount of motion.

Proposition XX.

If a body A meet a body B and they move on together the gain of motion in B and the loss of motion in A are equal.

DEMONSTRATION.

  If you deny it, let it be supposed that B acquires less motion from A than A loses. Then that quantity of motion must be added or substracted from the total motion in Nature, which is absurd (per Prop. 13 above). Since therefore, B can acquire neither more nor less motion than A loses it must receive just what is lost by A. Q. E. D.

Proposition XXI.

If a body A is twice as great as B and moves with an equal velocity, it will have twice the motion of B or a force for retaining a motion equal to that of B.

DEMONSTRATION.

Let it be supposed, for example, that in place of A there are two Bs that is (by hypothesis) A is divided into two equal parts. Each one then has the same inertia and (by hypothesis) the force in each is equal. If now these two parts are joined together their velocity remaining the same there will be a body A whose force and quantity will be equal to two Bs or double that of one B. Q. E. D.

This follows also from the definition of motion, for when a larger body is moved there is more matter separated from the surrounding matter. There is,

*therefore, more of a separation, that is (per Def. 8)
more motion. See also Def. VIII.*

PROPOSITION XXII.

*If a body A is equal to another body B and moves
with twice the velocity of B, the force or motion in A
is also double that of B. (Vid. Fig. Prop. 20).*

DEMONSTRATION.

Let it be supposed that B, when it first received a
certain force acquired a velocity of four degrees. If
it is not acted upon by some external force it will continue to move with the same velocity (per Prop. 14).
Suppose now, that by a new impulse it receives a new
force equal to that which it first received. It will
thus acquire four other degrees of velocity beside
those that it had before, which (per the same Prop.)
it will retain. Thus it will be moving with twice
its former velocity, or with the velocity of A, and
have double its former force or a force equal to that
of A. Therefore the motion in A is double that in B.
Q. E. D.

*It should be noted here, that by force (vis) we
understand the quantity of motion. This, in bodies of
equal size, will vary according to the velocity, for in a
given time the distance by which equal bodies are
separated from those tangent to them varies with the
velocity. Therefore those moving more swiftly have
more motion (per Def. 8). In bodies at rest by the
force of resistance we understand the quantity of rest.
From which follow:*

Corollary I.

The more slowly bodies move, the more they partake of rest, for bodies having a greater velocity meeting those which have less force, resist more and are not separated so far from bodies immediately contiguous to them.

Corollary II.

If a body A moves with double the velocity of a body B which is twice as large as A, they contain an equal amount of motion and force.

DEMONSTRATION.

If B is twice as large as A, but A moves with twice the velocity of B, and C is only half as large as B and moves only half as fast as A (per Prop. 21), B will have twice the force of C and A will have twice the motion of C (per Prop. 22). Therefore (per Ax. 15) B and A have an equal motion, for the motion of each is double that of the third body C. Q. E. D.

Corollary III.

From these corollaries it follows that motion must be distinguished from velocity. For we can conceive of bodies which have an equal velocity, but one of them having more motion than the other (per Prop. 21). And on the other hand, bodies with an unequal velocity may have an equal motion (per Coroll. II. above). This, also, is evident from the definition of motion which is nothing but the transference of one body from the vicinity, etc.

It should be noted that this corollary is not at vari-

ance with the first. For velocity is conceived in two ways: Either so far as a body in a given time is further or nearer removed from those bodies immediately contiguous to it, and so far partakes more or less of rest, or so far as in a given time it describes a longer or a shorter line and so far is distinguished from motion.

I might add other propositions to explain more fully Proposition 14, in regard to other points, as we have done in regard to motion. But it is sufficient to read Art. 43, Part II. of the Principles, and to add one Proposition only in order to understand what follows.

Proposition XXIII.

When the modes of a body are forced to suffer change, this change is always, under the circumstances, a minimum one.

DEMONSTRATION.

This proposition follows sufficiently clearly from Prop. 14.

Proposition XXIV—Rule 1.

If two bodies, for example A and B (vid. Fig. Prop. 20) are equal, and are moving toward one another with equal velocity, when they meet each will be reflected in an opposite direction without any loss of velocity.

In this hypothesis it is evident that in order that this opposition may be removed, either they must both be reflected in opposite directions or one must take the other on with it. For they are opposed only in regard to their determination, not as to their motion.

DEMONSTRATION.

Since A and B are mutually approaching one another they must suffer some change (per Ax. 19). But since the motion of the one is not opposed to the motion of the other (per Coroll. Prop. 19) they do not necessarily lose any of their motion (per Ax. 19). Therefore, the change is in their determination alone. But we can not say that the determination of only one, e. g. B, is changed unless A, by which it was changed, is supposed to be stronger (per Ax. 20). This, however, is contrary to the hypothesis. Therefore, since a change in the determination of only one is impossible, it will be in both, A and B being deflected in opposition directions (per what was said in ch. 2, Dioptric.), each retaining its original motion. Q. E. D.

Proposition XXV—Rule 2.

If they are unequal in mass, namely, B being greater than A (vid. Fig. Prop. 20) other things being as before, then A alone will be deflected and each will move with its former velocity.

DEMONSTRATION.

Since it is supposed that A is less than B, it will have less force than B. And, since in this hypothesis as in the last, the opposition is only in their determination, as we showed above, the variation therefore will be in their determination alone. It will be merely in A and not in B (per Ax. 20). Therefore, A alone will be reflected in an opposite direction by the greater body B, its former velocity being returned. Q. E. D.

Proposition XXVI.

If the mass and velocity are unequal, for example B twice as large as A (vid. Fig. Prop. 20), but A moving with double the velocity of B, other things being as before, both will be reflected in opposite directions, and each will retain its former velocity.

DEMONSTRATION.

Since A and B are moving toward one another, and according to hypothesis the motion in one is equal to that in the other (per Coroll. 2, Prop. 22); therefore, the motion of the one is not opposed to the motion of the other (per Coroll., Prop. 19). This hypothesis, therefore, is so far similar to the hypothesis of Proposition 24, and by the same demonstration A and B will be reflected in opposite directions by retaining each its former motion. Q. E. D.

COROLLARY.

From the three preceding Propositions it is evident that in order that a body be moved the determination of that body requires a force equal to its motion. Whence, it follows that a body which has lost more than half of its determination and more than half of its motion suffers more change than one which has lost all of its determination.

Proposition XXVII—Rule 3.

If A and B are equal in mass, but B moves a little more rapidly than A, not only is A reflected back in an opposite direction, but B gives to it one-half of its excess of motion, and both move in the same direction with an equal velocity.

A (by hypothesis) is opposed to B not only by its determination, but also by its slowness, so far as it partakes of the nature of rest (per Coroll., Prop. 22). Whence, although it is reflected in an opposite direction and its determination is changed, all of its opposition *(contrarietas)* is not destroyed. Therefore (per Ax. 19), there ought to be a variation both in its determination and in its motion. But since by hypothesis, B moves faster than A, B will have a greater force than A (per Prop. 22). Therefore, the change proceeds from B to A, which will be reflected in an opposite direction, which was the first point to be proved.

Then, so long as A moves more slowly than B, it will be opposed to B (per Coroll. 1, Prop. 22). Consequently there ought to be a variation in A until it moves with a velocity equal to B's (per Ax. 19). But in this hypothesis it is not impelled by some stronger force so that it should move more rapidly than B. Since it is impelled by B, it can not move slower than that body, nor can it move faster: therefore, it must move with a velocity equal to B's.

Further, if B gave less than one-half of its excess of velocity to A, A would move slower than B; if more than one-half, then faster, which as we have shown, is absurd. Therefore, the variation will continue until B has given one half of its excess of velocity to A, which B would therefore lose. So, also, they will both move without any opposition with an equal velocity in the same direction. Q. E. D.

COROLLARY.

It follows, that a body moving with a greater velocity has the more determination, so that it tends the more to move in a straight line; and, on the other hand, a body moving more slowly has less determination.

SCHOLIUM.

Lest the reader confuse the force of determination (vim determinationis) with the force of motion (vi motus), it seems best to explain these terms. If now the bodies A and C are equal, and are moving toward one another with an equal velocity, they will be deflected back (per Prop. 24), each retaining its former velocity. If there is a body C at B and it moves obliquely toward A its determination is less than its motion equaling the line B D or the line C A. Therefore, although the motion in the two cases is the same, the force of determination of C moving directly toward A is greater than the force of determination of C moving obliquely from B toward A in the ratio of AB to CA. Since it is here supposed that A and B move with an equal velocity, the time B consumes in moving from B to A or A C, which measures its opposition to A, will be to A's time as B A to A C. When the body C, moving from B along the line B A, strikes A, it will be deflected along the line of A B,' B' being on B C

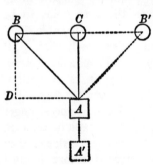

produced so that B′ C is equal to B C. And since the motion of the two bodies is equal the time B consumes in traversing the perpendicular distance A C is greater than the time of A in moving an equal distance or, to such a degree it is opposed to the determination of A, which is the stronger. In order that the determination of C moving from B toward A, may be equal to the determination of C (or from the hypothesis, to A), it is necessary that the motion from B be to the motion from C as B A is to C A. Then when it strikes the body A obliquely, A will be reflected back to A′ and B toward B′, each retaining its former velocity. But if B is as much greater than A as the line B A than C A, then B will repel A toward A′ and give of its motion until the motion of B is to the motion of A as the line B A is to C A, and by losing the motion which it has transferred to A it will proceed in the direction it was first moving. For example, if the line A C is to the line A B as 1 to 2, and the motion of A to the motion of B as 1 to 5, then B will give to A one degree of motion, and will repell it in an opposite direction, while B, having lost one-fifth of its motion, will move on in the same direction as before.

Proposition XXVIII—Rule 4.

If a body A (vid. Fig., Prop. 27), a little larger than B, is at rest, it will not be moved however great the velocity of B, but B will be deflected at an angle retaining its former motion.

Note.— Of these bodies there is opposition of three kinds: One when the one meets the other and they both move on with an equal velocity; the second when one is reflected in an opposite direction the other remaining at rest; the third when one is deflected from its course and gives some part of its motion to the body at rest. There is no fourth kind as is seen from Prop. 13. Therefore it will be evident (per Prop. 23) that conformable to our hypothesis the least possible change occurs in these bodies.

DEMONSTRATION.

If B moves A, until both move with the same velocity, it must give from its own motion (per Prop. 20) all that A acquires and consequently would lose more than half of its motion (per Prop. 21) as well as more than half of its determination (per Coroll., Prop. 27). So far (per Coroll., Prop. 26) it undergoes more change than if it lost all of its determination. And if A loses a part of its rest, but not so much that it moves with a velocity equal to B's, then the opposition of the two bodies is not destroyed. For A, so far as it partakes of rest, will be opposed to the motion of B, and so far B will be deflected from its course and will lose all of its determination and that part of its motion which it has given to A. And this also is a greater change than if it had lost its determination alone. The change, therefore, under our hypothesis, since it is in the determination alone, is the least possible that can come in these bodies, and therefore (per Prop. 23) the only possible one. Q. E. D.

It should be noted that in the demonstration of this Proposition, and it holds true likewise in other places, that we have not cited Prop. 19, where it was demonstrated, that the entire determination of a body may change, the motion remaining the same. Nevertheless this should be remembered in order that the force

of this argument may be seen. For in Prop. 23 we
do not say that the variation is the least absolutely,
but the least possible under the given conditions.
That such a change as this is possible, that is, a change
in the determination alone, is evident from Props. 18
and 19 with the Corollary.

PROPOSITION XXIX—Rule 5.

*If there is a body A, less than B, at rest (vid. Fig.
Prop. 30.), then, however slowly B moves toward A,
B will give such a portion of its motion to A that they
will move on together (Read Art. 50, Part II.
Principles).*

In this rule, as in the preceding, there are three
possible cases by which their opposition may be
destroyed. We will show that under this hypothesis
there is the least possible change in these bodies, and
so (per Prop. 23) this is the only variation.

DEMONSTRATION.

By hypothesis, B transfers to A (per Prop. 21) less
than half of its motion, and (per Coroll., Prop. 17)
less than half of its determination. But if B did not
carry A on with it, but should be reflected in an opposite direction, it would lose all of its determination
and there would be a greater variation (per Coroll.,
Prop. 26). And much greater even, if it should lose
all of its determination, and at the same time a part
of its motion, as is supposed in the third case.
Therefore, the change under our hypothesis is the
least possible. Q. E. D.

PROPOSITION XXX—Rule 6.

If a body A, at rest, is exactly equal to B, a body moving toward it, when B strikes A, A will be impelled and B repelled.

Here, as in the preceding, there are three possible cases, and we will show that the resulting change is the least possible.

DEMONSTRATION.

If the body B should take A with it until both move with an equal velocity, then the motion in each would be the same (per Prop. 22) and (per Coroll., Prop. 27) B would lose half of its determination and half of its motion   (per Prop. 20). If B is repelled in an opposite direction it will lose all of its determination but retain all its motion (per Prop. 18). In the latter case the change is equal to that of the former (per Coroll., Prop. 26). But neither of these is possible, for if A remains at rest and still changes the determination of B, it must needs (per Ax. 20) be greater than B, which is contrary to the hypothesis. And if B act on A until both move together with an equal velocity, B is greater than A, which is also contrary to the hypothesis. Since neither of these results is possible, the third case must be the result, namely, that B impels A a little, and is repelled by A. Q. E. D. Read Art. 51, Part II. of the *Principles*.

Proposition XXXI—Rule 7.

If B and A (vid. Fig. above) are moving in the same direction, A a little more slowly than B, which is following, so that it will impinge on A, and if A is greater than B, but the excess in magnitude is not equal to B's excess of velocity, then B will give a part of its velocity to A, so that they will move on together. But if the excess of motion in B does not equal the excess of magnitude in A, then B will be reflected back, each retaining its former velocity.

See Art. 52, Part of II. of the *Principles*. Here, as above, there are three possible cases.

DEMONSTRATION.

Point one: B, which is supposed to be stronger than A, cannot be reflected in an opposite direction (per Props. 21 and 22, and Ax. 20). Therefore, since B is stronger than A it will move A on with it so that the two advance together, for as appears from the previous proposition, there is less change in this way than in any other.

Point two: Since here B is not so strong as A it can not move A (per Props. 21 and 22), neither (per Ax. 20) can it give it any of its motion. Therefore (per Coroll., Prop. 14), it will retain its former motion. Not, however, in the same direction, for it is supposed to be impeded by A. Therefore (per what was said in Chap 2, Diopt.), it will be reflected in an opposite direction, each body retaining its former motion (per Prop. 18). Q. E. D.

It should be noted that here, as in the preceding propositions, we have assumed as proven that every body meeting another by which it is absolutely impeded, advances no further in its former direction, but on the contrary, is reflected in an opposite direction. To understand this read Chapter 2 of the *Diopts.*

SCHOLIUM.

For explaining the changes of bodies which are mutually impelled we have so far considered two bodies as though separated from all others, no account being taken of other impinging bodies. For we will consider the state and changes of those in place of the bodies by which they are impinged on all sides.

Proposition XXXII.

If a body B is impinged on all sides by moving particles which tend to move it in all directions, as long as there is no other cause it will remain unmoved.

DEMONSTRATION.

This proposition is self-evident: for if a body is moving from the impulse of corpuscles coming from a certain direction, the corpuscles which move it impel it with greater force than others coming from other parts, and striking it are unable to produce a sensible effect (per Ax. 20). But this is contrary to the hypothesis.

Proposition XXXIII.

Conditions being as in the last Proposition, a body B can be moved in a certain direction by a force however small.

DEMONSTRATION.

Since, by hypothesis, B is at rest, and the particles contiguous to it are in motion, these particles (per Prop. 28) in touching B are repelled, each one retaining its former velocity. B, therefore, is being continually left by those particles contiguous to it, and no action is required for separating it from those particles which come in contact with it (according to what was remarked concerning Def. 8). Therefore, however small the external force impinging on B, it is still greater than that required to retain B in its position (for we have shown that there is no force in the bodies immediately tangent to B), and which, added to the impact of the particles moving in the same direction, is not greater than the impact of particles moving in an opposite direction (for we suppose that these particles are acting equally on all sides.) Therefore (per Ax. 20), any external force, however small, will move B in a certain direction. Q. E. D.

Proposition XXXIV.

A body B, the conditions being as above, can not be moved with a velocity greater than the velocity of the body impelling it, although the particles of that body may be moving much more rapidly.

DEMONSTRATION.

The corpuscles which, together with the external force, impel B in a certain direction, although they move much more rapidly than the external force is able to move, nevertheless, since (by hypothesis) they have no greater force than those particles which tend to drive B in another direction, all strength of their determination is used in resisting these, and hence (per Prop. 32) they give no acceleration to the body. Therefore, since there are, according to supposition, no other elements or causes except this external force, nor does it receive acceleration from any other bodies except this external force, it can not be moved with a greater velocity than the impulse of this body. Q. E. D.

Proposition XXXV.

When a body B is so moved by an external force, it receives the greater part of its motion from those bodies which immediately surround it, and not from an external force.

DEMONSTRATION.

The body B, however large it is supposed to be, will be moved by the continued impulse of a body however small (per Prop. 33). Let us suppose that B is four times as large as an external body by which it is moved. Since (by the preceding Proposition) both will move with an equal velocity there will be four times as much motion in B as in the body by which it is impelled (per Prop. 21). Therefore (per Ax. 8, Part I.), it does not receive the principal part of its motion from this external force. And since no other factors are present except those bodies by which it is continually being impelled (for B is supposed to be at rest), it receives the greater part of its motion from these bodies continually acting upon it and not from some external force, Q. E. D.

Let it be noted here that we cannot say, as above,

that the motion of particles coming from one direction is needed to counterbalance the motion of parts coming from an opposite direction. For bodies moving toward one another (as is here supposed) with an equal motion are opposed to one another in their determination alone and not in their motion [1] (per Coroll. Prop. 19); hence when resisting one another they are opposed only in their determination and not in their motion. Beside B cannot receive from circumjacent bodies any determination and consequently no increase of velocity so far as it is distinguished from motion. It does, however, receive motion; therefore, some adventitious force being present, it must needs be moved by these particles as we have shown in this Proposition, and this is clear also from the method by which we demonstrate Proposition 33.

Proposition XXXVI.

If some body, for example my hand, moves with a uniform motion in any direction so that it in no way resists any bodies, nor do any bodies in any way resist it, in the space through which it moves the bodies must necessarily be moving in all directions and with a velocity equal to that of my hand.

DEMONSTRATION.

A body can move through no space that is not a plenum (per Prop. 3). That is, the space through which my hand is moving is filled with bodies which move under the condition given above. If you deny

---

[1] See Proposition 24 of this book, where it was demonstrated that bodies resisting one another are opposed only in their determination and not in their motion.

it let it be supposed that they are at rest or are moving in some other way. If they were at rest they necessarily resist the motion of the hand (per Prop. 14) until its motion is communicated to them so that they move in the same direction and with a velocity equal to that of my hand (per Prop. 20). But it is supposed in the hypothesis that they do not resist. Therefore, they are moving, which is the first point to be proved. These bodies must be moving in all directions. If you deny it let it be supposed that they do not move in one direction, say from A to B. If, therefore, the hand is moving from A to B it will necessarily meet with moving particles (according to what has just been said and according to hypothesis) with a different determination from the determination of the hand. Therefore, they would resist it (per Prop. 14) until they are moved in the same direction as the hand itself (per Prop. 24 and Schol. Prop. 27). And since (by hypothesis) they do not resist the hand, they will be moving in the same direction, which was the second point.

Again, these bodies in whatever direction they move, will all have an equal velocity. For if it be supposed that they do not move with an equal velocity, let it be supposed that those which move from A toward B, do not have as great a velocity as those which move from A toward C.

Therefore, if the hand moves from A to B with the same velocity as the bodies moving from A to C (for it is supposed to be able to move with an equal velocity in any direction without resistance), the bodies moving from A toward B will resist the hand until they move with the hand with an equal velocity (per Props. 14 and 31). But this is contrary to hypothesis. Therefore they will move in all directions with an equal velocity, which was the third point.

Finally, if these bodies do not move with an equal velocity to the hand, the hand moves either slower or faster than they. If the former the hand would resist the bodies which are following it in the same direction (per Prop. 31); if these particles move slower than the hand, then they will resist the hand, both cases being contrary to our hypothesis. Therefore, since the hand does not move slower or faster than the particles it must move with a velocity equal to that of the particles amid which it moves. Q. E. D.

If you inquire why with an equal degree of velocity, I would reply that it is not with a velocity absolutely equal. See Schol. Coroll. Prop. 27. If then you would ask whether the hand while, for example, it was moving from A to B would not resist those particles at that time moving from B to A, read Prop. 33, in which you will see that the force of these bodies is equalized by the force of bodies moving from A to B (for by the third part of this demonstration this force is equal to that).

Proposition XXXVII.

If some body, A for example, can be moved in a certain direction by a force however small, it is necessarily surrounded by bodies which are all moving with equal velocity in all directions.

DEMONSTRATION.

This body A is surrounded on all sides by bodies (per Prop. 6), which are moving in all directions with an equal velocity. For if they were at rest the body A (as is supposed), could not be moved in a given direction by a force however small, but only by a minimum force which was able to move A together with the bodies which immediately surround it (per Ax. 20). Then if the bodies by which A is surrounded are moved in one direction with a greater force than in another, for example, from B to C than from C to B, since as we have already shown it is ④ C———— B surrounded on all sides by moving bodies, it will necessarily be moved along the line from B to C (per Prop. 30). Hence a force however small would not suffice to move A from C to B, but one sufficient to overcome this excess of motion toward B would be required (Ax. 20). Therefore these bodies must be moving in all directions with an equal force.

SCHOLIUM.

Since these things are true of fluid bodies, it follows that fluid bodies are those which are divided into minute parts, which are moving in all directions with equal velocity. And, although these particles cannot be seen even by the eye of a lynx, still the truth of what we have thus demonstrated cannot be denied. For, in Propositions 10 and 11 it was shown that the subtlety of nature is so great that it cannot be known (I shall not say by the senses). Beside, as was also shown above, since bodies only by their rest resist other bodies, and as the senses tell us hardness is nothing else than the resistance the parts of a body offer to our hands, we conclude that those bodies are hard whose particles are, with regard to another at rest, and near together.

Read Articles 54, 55, and 56, Part II. Prin.

The Principles of Philosophy Demonstrated by the Method of Geometry.

PART III.

The universal principles of nature having been presented, we must proceed now to explain those things which follow from them. But since the things which follow from these principles are more than can ever be known, and since we are not determined by them to one thing rather than another, first of all a brief history should be given of the principal phenomena whose causes we are to investigate. This you have in Articles 5 to 15, Part III. of the *Principles*. And from Articles 20 to 40 the hypothesis is expressed which Descartes deemed best fitted not only to explain the phenomena of the world, but also for investigating their natural causes.

The best way to understand the nature of plants or of men is to see how they arise and develop from their germ cells. Principles perfectly simple and easily known should be found from which we can demonstrate that the heavens, the earth, and all the visible world could have arisen as from cells, although we know full well that they have not actually done so. For in this way we will explain their nature much better than if we only describe them.

I say that we are seeking for principles which are simple and easily known. Unless such are found we do not desire any at all. For we are only adding the first principles to what has been given in order that the nature of these things may more easily be known, and that we may, according to the method of mathematics, advance from what is perfectly clear to that which is more obscure, and from the simple to what is more complex.

Therefore, we said that we are seeking the principles from which we might demonstrate that the heavens, the earth, etc., could have arisen. We are not seeking merely the causes which are sufficient, for explaining the phenomena of the heavens as is now and then done by astronomers. But we are seeking for those principles which will lead us to a knowledge of all those things in the earth (for we believe that all those things which we observe in the earth should be included in the phenomena of nature). In order that these may be found, the following points should be observed in a valid hypothesis:

I.   That (considered in itself alone), it implies no contradiction.

II.   That it should be as simple as possible.

III.   That what follows from it may be easily known.

IV.   That all things observed in all nature can be deduced from it.

Finally, we said, that we might assume an hypothesis from which, as from a cause we are able to deduce the phenomena of nature although we know that these phenomena have not thus arisen. In order that this may be understood I will give an example. If a person should find on a paper the curved line which we call a parabola and wished to investigate its nature it would make no difference whether he regarded it as first cut from some cone and then placed upon the paper, or whether he regarded it as generated from the movement of two straight lines, or as derived in some other way. In whatever way he conceives it to have been generated, he wishes to demonstrate all the properties of the parabola from it. Indeed, although he knows that it was made from the cone, he will be free to assign some other cause which seems to him better adapted to explain all its properties. So also in order to explain the forms of nature we may assume any hypothesis at will, provided we deduce from it, through mathematical inference, all the phenomena of nature. And, what is even more worthy of note, we can scarcely assume anything, from which we may not, perhaps with more labor, through the laws of nature given above, deduce the same results. For since in accordance with these laws, matter assumes successively all the forms of which it is capable, if we consider these forms in order we will come finally to the form in which the world exists. We need not fear, therefore, the error of a false hypothesis.

A POSTULATE.

We ask that it be conceded that, in the beginning, all matter of which the visible world is composed was divided by God into particles as nearly as possible equal to one another. These particles, however, from which now the heavens and the stars are composed were not spherical, for a number of spheres joined together do not fill up the space they occupy; but they, small in size, were fashioned in some other way. These particles had in them just as much motion as there is in the world to-day and they were all moving with an equal velocity. Not only did single particles mutually separate from one another move about their own center as if they composed a fluid body, such as we think the heavens to be, but there are many moving together around certain other points, equally remote and like disposed and now the centers of fixed bodies; then also, there were some around other points which equal the number of the planets. And so they compose as many vortices as there are stars in the world. Vid. Fig. Art. 47, Part III. of the *Principles*.

This hypothesis considered in itself implies no contradiction; for it attributes nothing to matter except divisibility and motion, which we have already demonstrated to really exist in matter. And since we have shown that matter is indefinite, and the earth and the heavens are one and the same, we can suppose without a trace of contradiction, that these modifications are in all matter.

Then this hypothesis is a very simple one, because there is no irregularity or dissimilarity in the particles into which matter was divided at the beginning, nor in their motion. For these reasons this hypothesis is also very easy to understand. This is evident also from the fact that in this hypothesis nothing is assigned to matter except that which is known to any one from the concept of matter alone, namely, divisibility and motion in space.

We shall attempt to show, as far as it may be done and in the following order, that all that we observe in nature can be deduced from this alone. In the first place we will deduce the fluidity of the heavens from this postulate and explain how this is the cause of light. Then we shall proceed to consider the nature of the sun and those things which are observed in

the fixed stars. Afterward we shall speak of comets
and of the planets and their phenomena.

DEFINITIONS.

I. By the *Equator* (per Eclipticam) we understand
that part of a rotating body, which as it turns on its
axis, describes the greatest circle.

II. By the *Poles* we understand those parts of a
rotating body most remote from the Equator, or which
describe minimum circles.

III. By the *Conatus to move* (conatum ad motum)
we do not understand some form of thought, but only
that a part of matter is so placed and impelled to
move that, if it is not impeded by some external cause,
it will really move somewhere.

IV. By an *Angle* we understand that part of a body
which extends beyond its spherical form.

AXIOMS.

I. A number of spheres joined together cannot fill
the space they occupy.

II. A portion of matter divided into angular parts
requires more space, if these parts each move about
its own center, than if they are all at rest and the sides
of all are immediately and mutually tangent to one
another.

III. A smaller part of matter is easier divided by
a given force than a larger one.

IV. Parts of matter moving in the same direction
which do not in this motion recede from one another,
are not really divided.

PROPOSITION I.

The parts into which matter was first divided are not spherical but angular.

DEMONSTRATION.

In the beginning all matter was divided into equal and similar parts (per Postulate). Therefore (per Ax. 1 and Prop. 2, Part II.) they are not spherical but (per Def. 4) thus far angular. Q. E. D.

PROPOSITION II.

The force which causes the particles of matter to move about their own centers, also causes the angles of these particles to be worn away.

DEMONSTRATION.

In the beginning all matter was divided into equal and angular parts, (per Postulate and Prop. 1). If the angles were not worn away when they began to move around their centers, all matter would occupy (per Ax. 2) more space than if they were at rest. But this is absurd (per Prop. IV., Part II). Therefore their angles begin to wear away as soon as they began to move. Q. E. D.

APPENDIX

CONTAINING

COGITATA METAPHYSICA,

In which are briefly discussed some questions
and difficulties which occur in regard to
Being and. its Affects, God and His
Attributes, and the Human
Mind.

BY

BENEDICTUS DE SPINOZA,

Amsterdam.

APPENDIX

COGITATA METAPHYSICA.

Part I,

In which some points relating to Being and its Affects are briefly explained.

Chapter I.

Concerning Real Being, Fictitious Being, and Being of Reason.

Concerning the definition of knowledge (Scientia) I shall say nothing, not even of the knowledge of the things here discussed. I shall only attempt to explain some obscure points in those authors who write on Metaphysics.

Definition of Being.

We shall begin, therefore, with Being, by which I mean, *all of that which, when it is clearly and distinctly conceived is found to exist necessarily, or at least to be able to exist.*

Chimeras, fictitious being, and being of reason are not real.

From this definition, or, if you prefer, from this description, it follows that chimeras, fictitious being and being of the reason can in no way be called real. For chimeras [1] by their nature do not

[1] By chimera is understood a being which by nature involves a contradiction as is clearly shown in Chapter III.

exist. Fictitious being precludes any clear and distinct concept, because man by his mere power of Freedom, not unknowingly as in false concepts, but advisedly and intelligently, connects what he wishes to connect, and dissociates what he will. Finally, being of reason is nothing except a mode of thought which pertains most properly to the intellect, viz., to retention, to understanding, and to the imagination. It should here be noted that by mode of thought we mean, as was explained in Schol. Prop. Pt. I., all forms of mental states as understanding, joy, imagination, etc.

In what way objects are retained in memory. That there are certain modes of thought which serve the purpose of retaining objects firmly in the mind, and of recalling them when we wish, is evident to all who use the well-known rule of memory; viz., that by which, for retaining anything in memory and impressing it upon the mind, it is associated with some other thing familiar to us, either by name, or because of its contiguity with that object. In this way philosophers have reduced all natural objects to certain classes called *genera, species,* etc., and to these they refer all new objects as they are met.

In what way we explain objects. Then, for explaining things we have also modes of thought derived by comparing one object with another. Such modes as these are time, number, measure, etc. Of these time serves for explaining duration, number for discrete quantities, and measure for continuous quantity.

In what way we imagine things. Finally since we have become accustomed to picture all of those things which we understand, even the images of our fancy at times, it happens that we imagine non-being positively, as an image of some real being. For mind considered as a thinking being has no more power to affirm than to deny. And since to imagine is only to perceive the traces in the brain produced by the movement of the spirits, which in turn are caused by the stimulation of the senses by an external object, such a sensation can only be a confused affirmation. Hence we imagine all the forms of thought which the mind uses for denying as *blindness*, the *limits* or *termini*, the *end, shade,* etc., are beings.

Why beings of reason are not ideas of things but are so considered. It is thus evident that such modes of thought are not ideas of things, nor can they, in any possible way, be so considered. They have no object, which necessarily exists, as the source of the idea, nor could such an object possibly exist. The reason such forms of thought are so often held for ideas of things is that they arise so directly from real things, that those who do not very carefully attend to their thought readily confuse such forms of thought with the things themselves. For this cause also, they give names to these ideas as if they signified some real extra-mental object, which being, or rather non-being, they call beings of the reason.

It is not correct to divide Being into real being and being of reason. It is easy to see how inapt is the division which divides Being into real being and being of the reason. For they divide Being into being and non-being or into being and a mode of thought. However, I do not wonder that philosophers sometimes fall into these verbal or grammatical errors. For they judge objects from the names and not names from the objects.

In what sense being of the reason may be called nothing, and in what sense real. Those who say that being of the reason is *nothing*, however, are not less in error. If you seek for some meaning for these terms apart from the mind you find nothing; but if we understand by the term a mode of thought, then it signifies something real. For if I ask what a *species* is, I only inquire for the nature of that form of thought as something real and to be distinguished from other modes. These modes of thought, moreover, cannot be called ideas, nor can they be said to be true or false, just as love, e. g., cannot be called true or false but only good or evil. So when Plato said that " man is a biped without feathers," he did not err more than if he had said that man is a rational animal. For Plato knew that man was a rational animal as well as he knew the other. He merely put man into a certain class, so that when he wished to reflect upon man by recurring to the class in which he had been classified he would come immediately to recognize certain characteristics as belonging to his nature. Aristotle, indeed, made a grave mistake if he thought that Plato in this definition attempted to express the essence of human nature. Whether Plato did well we may question, but this is not the place to discuss that.

In our investigation of things, real being must not be confused with being of reason. From all that has been said above it appears that there is no conformity between real being and being of reason. Therefore, it is easily seen how seduously we must be on our guard lest we confuse the two. For it is one thing to inquire into the nature of things and quite another to inquire into the nature of the modes of thought under which they are perceived. If we do not keep this distinction clear we

will be unable to understand modes of perception, or
the nature of things in themselves. But what is more
important, since this affects so many things, is that
this is the reason we often fall into such great error.

*In what way being
of reason and
fictitious being
are distinguish-
able.*
It should be noted also that many
confuse being of reason and fictitious
being. They think that the one is
equal to the other because neither has
an extra-mental existence. But if they would consider the definitions of each, great and important differences would be found, not only in respect to their
cause, but in their nature apart from their cause.

For we affirm that fictitious being is nothing but
two terms connected by the mere act of volition without any dependence upon reason. Being of reason
does not depend upon the will alone nor is it formed
by terms, as is evident without a rational connection
between them, from the definition itself. If one should
ask, therefore, whether fictitious being, or being of
reason is real it should be answered that it is wrong
to divide all being into real being and being of reason.
The question is fundamentally wrong for it presupposes that all being is divided into real being and being
of reason.

*The division of
Being.*
But to return to the proposition
from which we seem to have digressed.
From the definition of Being or, if you prefer, from its
description, it is now easily seen that Being should not
be divided into Being which, because of its own nature
necessarily exists, or Being whose essence involves
existence, and into Being whose essence involves only
a possible existence. This last is divided into Substance and Modes, the definitions of which are given in
the *Principles of Phil.,* Pt. I., Articles 51, 52 and 56.

We need not, therefore, repeat them here. In regard to this, however, and I say it deliberately, I wish it to be noted that Being is divided into Substance and Modes, not into Substance and Accidents. For Accident is nothing but a mode of thought and exists only in regard to this. For example, when I say that a triangle is moved the motion is not a mode of the triangle but of the body moved. Therefore, in respect to the triangle motion is only an accident but in respect to the body it is real being or mode; for motion cannot be conceived without a body but it may without a triangle.

Further, in order that we may the better understand what has been said and what is to follow, we will attempt to explain briefly what is meant by the terms *essence, existence, idea,* and *power.* We are the more urged to do this by the ignorance of those who do not recognize the distinction between essence and existence, or if they do recognize it still confuse the terms essence with the terms idea or power. Therefore, in order to help them and to make the matter plain we attempt to explain this as clearly as possible.

CHAPTER II.

What should be understood by the terms Essence, Existence, Idea and Power.

In order that it may be known what content to give to these four terms, it is necessary that we should understand clearly what may be said of uncreated substance, or God. Namely:

1. That God eminently contains **All created things are eminently contained in God.** all that is formally contained in created things, that is, God has certain attributes in which these created things are more eminently contained than in the things themselves. (Vid. Pt. I. Ax. 8, and Coroll. I. Prop. 12). For example, we can clearly conceive of extension without existing objects, and thus, since it has no power of existence in itself, we have shown that it was created by God (Prop. 21, Pt. I.). And, since there must be as much perfection in the cause as there is in the effect, it follows that God contains all the perfection of existence. But since we find later that extended matter is divisible, that is, that it contains a mark of imperfection, we cannot, therefore, attribute extension to God. We are thus compelled to admit that God has some attribute more excellent than all the perfection of matter and thus contains (Schol. Prop. 9, Pt. I.) what the defects of matter cannot supply.

2. God understands Himself and all other objects; that is, He holds all things objectively, in Himself (Pt. I. Prop. 9).

3. God is the first cause of all things, and works from an absolute freedom of will.

What should be understood by essence, existence idea and power. From these things it is evident what we must understand by these four terms. In the first place *Essence* in nothing else than that mode by which created objects are comprehended in the attributes of God; an idea is Idea so far as all things are objectively contained in the idea of God; *Power* is so called in respect to the power of God, by which, by an absolute freedom of will He was able to create everything that exists; finally, existence is the essence of things apart from God, and, considered in itself alone, is attributed to things after they have been created by God.

These four terms are not distinguished the one from the other except in created objects.
From this it is evident that these four terms are not to be distinguished except in created objects; in God, in no way can they be differentiated. For we cannot conceive that God is in the power of another, and His existence, and His understanding are not to be separated from His essence.

A reply to certain questions concerning God's Essence.
From what has been said we can readily reply to certain questions which have been asked. Such, for example, are the following: *Whether essence is different from existence; and if different, is it something diverse from idea; and if different from idea, does it comprehend something extra-mental;* which last follows from necessity. To the first in regard to distinction we would reply, that essence in God is not different from existence, indeed the one cannot be conceived without the other. In other things essence differs from existence, for the one may be conceived without the other. To the second point we respond, that things which can be clearly and distinctly conceived as extra-mental are something different from idea. But then it is asked, *whether that which is extra-mental exists in itself alone, or whether it has been created by God.* To this we reply, that formal essence does not exist by its own power, nor even when created. These two conditions presuppose that the object exists in fact; but they depend upon the divine essence alone, in which all things are contained. So far we would assent to the opinion of

those who affirm that the essence of things is eternal. Again it may be asked, *How can we understand the essence of things, when God's nature is not yet known;* for all things, as we have just said, depend upon the nature of God. To this I reply that it is possible from the fact that things are now actually created. For if things were not yet created I would concede that it would be impossible until we had an adequate knowledge of God's nature. In the same way it is impossible, indeed more impossible then for us to know the orderly nature of the applications of a parabola whose nature is not yet known.

Why the author in his definition of essence refers to the attributes of God. Although the essence of non-existing modes is comprehended in the substance of these modes, and their real essence is these substances, nevertheless we desire to refer them to God in order to explain the essence of modes and of substances in general terms, and because the essence of modes was not in substance prior to creation and we are seeking for an eternal essence.

Why the definitions of others are not examined. I do not think it worth while to refute those authors who think differently from us, or even to examine their definitions or descriptions of essence and existence; this would only make what is clear more obscure. What, indeed, is better known than the meaning of essence or existence? How can we give a definition of anything which does not at the same time explain its essence?

How the distinction between essence and existence can easily be seen. Finally, if any philosopher is yet in doubt whether essence and existence are distinguishable in created objects, he need not take much trouble to remove that doubt. For if he will merely approach some statue or object of wood, he will see how he conceives of the object not yet existing in a certain manner, and how he knows that it is really existing.

CHAPTER III.

Concerning those things which are Necessary, Impossible, Possible, and Contingent.

What is here understood by the Affects The nature of being as being having been explained we would next consider some of its affects. It may be remarked here, that by *affects* we understand what Descartes termed *attributes* (Pt. I. Prin. Phil. Art. 52). For being, considered merely as being does not affect us as substance. Wherefore it must be explained by some attribute which is recognized only by reason. Wherefore I cannot wonder enough, at the extreme subtlety of those who, not without deleterious consequences to truth, try to find some middle ground between being and nothing. But I will not delay to refute this error, seeing that it fades into their own vain subtlety when they attempt to give a definition of the affects.

Definition of the Affects. We then take up the matter at once and say: *The affects of being are certain attributes under which we come to understand the essence or existence of every single thing, which attributes, however, are only distinguishable by reason.* I shall attempt here to explain certain things about these (for I do not assume that all understand this thoroughly) and to separate by proper terms those things which are not the affects of being.

First I shall discuss what is meant by *necessary* and *impossible.*

In how many ways a thing may be said to be necessary or impossible. There are two ways in which a thing may be said to be necessary or impossible, viz., in respect to its essence or its cause. In respect to His essence we know that God necessarily exists. For His essence cannot be conceived without existence. From the implicated essence of chimeras they cannot exist. In respect to their cause, things, i. e., materials, are either impossible or necessary. For if we merely regard their essence, it is possible to clearly conceive of that without their existence. Therefore, they cannot exist by the power and necessity of their own essence but only by the power of their cause, viz., God the creator of all things. If, thus, it is the divine decree that something should exist, it exists from necessity, or if less than this, it will be impossible for it to exist. For it is a self-evident fact that that which has no cause, internal or external, for its existence, cannot possibly exist. And an object under this hypothesis is so conceived that it cannot exist by the power of its own essence, by which I mean an internal cause, nor by the divine decree, the one external cause of all things. Whence it follows that objects under such condition cannot exist at all.

A chimera is rightly called a mere verbal being. It should be noted: 1. A chimera because it exists neither in the intellect nor in the imagination is rightly called a mere verbal being; for we can only express this idea in words. For example, we use the words "a square circle," expressing it in words, but we are by no means able to imagine it, much less to understand it. Therefore chimera is only a word and cannot be numbered among the affects of being.

2. We must remember that not only *Created objects derive their essence and existence from God.* does the existence of all created things depend upon God's decree, but their essence and nature as well. This will be clearly shown in Part II. below. Whence it follows that created objects have no necessity in themselves, for their essence is not self derived. No more do they exist by their own power.

3. Finally, it should be noted that *The necessity in created objects is derived from their cause, and relates to their essence or existence. In God these two things are not to be distinguished.* the necessity of created objects, such as we find there from the power of the cause, is either in respect to their essence or to their extension. These two must be distinguished in created objects. The one depends upon the eternal laws of nature, the other upon the series and the order of its causes. In God whose essence and existence are the same, necessity of essence is equivalent to necessity of existence. Whence it follows that if we conceive of the *whole order of Nature* we will find that many things cannot exist whose nature we conceive clearly and distinctly, that is, whose nature is such of necessity. For we find that it is equally impossible for such things to be, as for example we know that it is impossible for a great elephant to pass through the eye of a needle. Nevertheless the nature of each is clearly conceived.

Therefore things of this nature do not exist except chimeras, which we are able neither to imagine nor to understand.

So much concerning necessity and *Possibility and con-* impossibility; to which it seems best *tingency are not* *affects of things.* to add a few remarks concerning what is *possible* and what is *contingent.*
For by some, these two terms are considered affects of things, although, in truth, they are nothing more than defects of our intellect. This I shall clearly show after I have explained what should be understood by these terms.

What is possible, *A thing is said to be possible when* *what is contin-* *we understand its efficient cause, but* *gent.* *do not know whether it is determined.*
Therefore, we may consider that to be possible which is neither necessary or impossible. If now we attend merely to the essence of a thing and not to its cause, we say it is contingent; that is, when we consider any things between the extremes God and chimeras. This is true, for from a part of their essence we find no necessity of existence in these things as in God, nor impossibility of existence as in chimeras. If any one wishes to call that contingent which I call possible and possible what I call contingent I shall not contradict him. For I am not accustomed to dispute about mere names. It will be sufficient if it is only admitted that these arise not because of something real, but only because of defects of our perception.

Possible and con- If any one chooses to deny this his *tingent only sig-* error may be pointed out with little *nify defects in* *our understand-* trouble. For if he will consider Na- *ing.* ture and how it all depends upon God, he will find nothing *contingent.* That is, he will find nothing, which, from a part of the object is able to exist and not exist, or, as it is generally expressed, the contingent is the real. This is evident, also, from what was said in Ax. 10, Pt. I. namely, that no more power was needed to create the world than to conserve it. Therefore no created object does anything by its own power for the same reason that it did not begin to exist by its own power. From which it follows that nothing has been created except by the power of the Cause which has created all things, namely, the power of God, who by His concurrence procreates everything every single moment. And since nothing exists except by divine power alone, it is easily seen that the world as produced by God's decree is such as he wished it to be. So, too, since there is no change or inconstancy in God (per Prop. 18 and Coroll. Prop. 20, Pt. I.), those things which He now produces, He has decreed from eternity that they should be produced. Then since nothing more is needed for their existence than God's decree that they should exist, it follows that the necessity of the existence of all created things has existed from eternity. Nor can we say that these things are contingent since God might have decreed otherwise. For since in eternity there are no effects of time neither a future nor a past, it follows that God did not exist before that decree, so that he was able to decree something else.

The reconciliation of our Freedom with the predestination of God's will surpasses human understanding. Whatever pertains to the freedom of the human will, which we have said is free (Schol. Prop. 15, Pt. I.), that also is conserved by the concurrence of God. Nor is there any man who wishes or does anything who does not do as God has decreed from eternity that he should choose or act. In what way this is possible, human freedom being preserved, man is unable to understand. Since we clearly conceive this, our ignorance of how it can be should not lead us to reject this truth. For we clearly and distinctly understand, if we consider our nature, that we are free in our actions, and we deliberate about many things simply because we choose to do so. And on the other hand if we consider the nature of God in the way we have indicated, we see clearly and distinctly that all things depend upon Him and that nothing exists except as it has been decreed from all eternity. In what way the human will can be thus procreated by God so that it retains its freedom, we do not know. Indeed, there are many things which surpass our comprehension, and yet we know that they are so ordained by God; as for example, that there is a real division of matter into indefinite parts, which was sufficiently proven in Proposition 11, Part II. although we do not understand how such a division can be. These two motions, viz., *possible* and *contingent*, which we use in place of the thing known, only signify a defect of our knowledge about the existence of the given object.

CHAPTER IV.

Concerning Duration and Time.

What Eternity is. Because above, we have divided being into being whose essence involves existence, and being whose essence involves only a possible existence, there arises the distinction between eternity and duration. Concerning eternity we will speak at length below. Here we would only say that it is an *attribute under which we conceive the infinite existence of God. Duration is* *What Duration is. an attribute under which we conceive*

*the existence of created objects so far as they perse-
vere in their own actuality.*

What Time is.   From which it clearly follows that
duration is distinguished from the
whole existence of an object only by the reason. For,
however much of duration you take away from any
thing, so much of its existence do you detract from it.
In order to determine or measure this we compare this
with the duration of those objects which have a fixed
and a certain motion, *and this comparison is called time.*
Therefore, time is not an affect of things but only a
mode of thought or, as we have said, a being of reason; it is a mode of thought serving to explain duration. It should be noted under duration, as it will be
of use when below we are discussing eternity, that it is
conceived as greater or less, as it were, composed of
parts and then not only as an attribute of existence
but as the very essence of existence.

Chapter V.

Concerning Opposition, Order, etc.

Because we compare objects one with another, there
are certain notions that arise, which, however apart
from the things themselves are only modes of thought.
This is very evident, since, when we attempt to consider them as objects apart from forms of thought
we hold the one for the other and render clear concepts obscure. Such notions are the following, viz.,
Opposition, Order, Relation, Diversity, Connection,
Conjunction, and other similar ideas. These, I say,
are perceived by us with sufficient clearness provided
we do not conceive of them as something in the essence

of things, but only as modes of thought by which we can more easily retain these objects in memory and imagine them. Therefore, I do not think it necessary to speak further of this but pass to those terms commonly called transcendental.

CHAPTER VI.

Concerning Unity, Truth and Goodness.

By almost all metaphysicians these terms are held to be affects of being. For, they say, all being is one, true and good, although no one knows about this. By examining each one of these terms separately we shall be able to understand their proper use.

What Unity is. We will begin with the first, viz., *Unity.* This term, they say, signifies some extra-mental reality. But what this adds to reality they are unable to say. Which sufficiently shows that they confuse being of reason with real being, so that what is perfectly clear becomes obscure. We, on the other hand, would say that unity is in no way to be distinguished from the thing itself, and that it adds nothing to being. But it is only a mode of thought by which we separate one thing from another, when they are similar or for some reason occur together

What Plurality is, and in what sense God may be said to be ONE, and in what sense sui generis. To the term *Unity* we oppose the term *Plurality*, which clearly adds nothing to things but is only a mode of thought which assists us in understanding the objects of our experience.

Nor do I see that anything remains to be said concerning a matter as self-evident as this.

We may add, however, that God so far as we separate Him from other objects may be said to be one. But so far as we think of His nature as many-sided He cannot be called simple Unity (unum et unicum). If we examine the matter more accurately, we can show that God is improperly called simple unity. But this is not of sufficient importance to make it worth the discussion; it is a matter that affects not the reality but the names. Therefore we pass to the second point and explain what we mean by ' false.'

What is true and what is false, as generally understood and as understood by philosophers. In order to properly understand the terms *true* and *false* we will begin with their signification from which it will appear that they are not names of qualities in the things themselves nor attributes at all except rhetorically. Since general usage first fixed their meaning, and they were only used afterward by philosophers, it seems best to inquire for their primary significance. Especially is this necessary since other sources from the very nature of language, are wanting. The significance of *true* and *false* seemed to have first arisen from narration. That narration was true which was in accord with the facts which it concerned; that was false which was not in accord with the facts of the case. This use of these terms was then borrowed by philosophers for denoting the correspondence of the idea with the thing it represents, and the contrary. Therefore, that idea is said to be true which represents the thing, as it is in itself. That idea is false which does not so represent its object. For ideas are nothing else than mental narratives or histories of nature. Afterward these are metaphorically applied to other things. As for example, that gold is true or

false, as if we thought that gold which we perceive
might tell us what was in itself, or what is not.

is not a ,cendental trans. Wherefore those who believe that
true is a transcendental term, or an
affect of being, are plainly deceived.
For we only apply this term to *things* improperly, or
if ou prefer, rhetorically.

How Truth and a true idea differ. If you inquire further what truth
is but a true idea, you do the same
thing as to ask what whiteness is except a white object.

Concerning the cause of the true and the false we
have already spoken; therefore nothing remains to be
noted which would be worth the while, if writers,
"seeking a knot in the bulrushes," did not so far en-
tangle themselves in similar folly that they are unable
to extricate themselves.

What are the Prop- erties of Truth? Certitude is not in things. The properties of truth or of a true
idea are: 1. That it is clear and dis-
tinct. 2. That it is beyond all doubt,
or, in a word, that it is certain. Those
who seek for certainty in the things themselves are
deceived in the same way as when they seek there for
truth. Although we say a *thing is uncertain,* we rhetorically take the object for the idea, and in the same
way we say that a thing is doubtful. Unless, perchance, we understand by uncertainty, contingency or
the thing which makes us uncertain or doubtful. But
there is no need to delay about this point. Therefore
we proceed to the third point and will explain what is
meant by this term and its opposite.

Good and Evil only relative terms. An object considered in itself is
neither good nor evil, but only in re-
spect to another being, which it helps

to acquire what is desired, or the contrary. Indeed, the same thing at the same time may be both good and evil in respect to different things. For example, the council of Ahithophel to Absalom is called good in the Sacred Scriptures. But it was the worst possible to David, whose destruction it would have caused. So there are many things which are good, but not good for all. Health is good for man, but neither good nor evil to senseless matter or to plants, to which it does not apply. God is called perfectly good because He preserves all things. He conserves all things by His concurrence, and no greater mark of goodness could be found than this. Nor is there any absolute evil, as is also evident in itself.

Why some conceive of a metaphysical Good. Those who seek for some metaphysical good which shall be free from relativity are laboring under a misapprehension of the case. They confuse a distinction of Reason with a distinction of Reality or Modality. They distinguish between the thing itself, and its *conatus,* by which each object is conserved, although they do not know what they mean by the term *conatus.* For these two things, although they are distinguished by reason, or by words, which fact deceives them, are not to be distinguished in the thing itself.

How the thing itself, and the conatus by which every object endeavors to conserve itself in its present state, are to be distinguished. In order to understand this we will notice a very simple example. Motion has the power of preserving itself *in statu quo;* this power clearly is nothing else than the motion itself, i. e., it is in the nature of motion to do so. If I say that in A there is nothing else than a certain amount of motion, it follows that as long as I consider only this body A, I must consider it as moving. For if I should say that it has lost its power of motion, I necessarily attribute something else to it than that which, from the hypothesis, it possessed, and through this, it has lost its power of motion. If this reason seems obscure — well then we will concede that this conatus of self-movement is something more than the laws and nature of motion. If, therefore, you suppose this conatus to be a metaphysical good, from necessity you must suppose that this conatus will have in it a conatus of self-preservation, and this another, and so on to infinity, than which I do not know anything more absurd. The reason some distinguish between the conatus of an object and the thing itself is this, namely, because they find in themselves the desire of conserving themselves, they imagine the desire is present in everything.

Whether God could have been called good, before creation. Moreover, it is asked whether God could have been called good before creation. From our definition it would seem that we could not predicate such an attribute as belonging to God, for we said that a thing considered in itself alone can neither be said to be good or evil. This will seem absurd to many; but for what reason I do not know. We attribute many things of this kind to God, which, before creation, could not exist except potentially; as for example, when He is called Creator, Judge merciful, etc. Wherefore similar arguments should be allowed us here.

In what sense Perfection is relative, in what sense absolute. And further, as good and evil are only relative terms, so also is perfection, unless we take perfection for the essence of the thing; in this sense, as we have said before, God has infinite perfection, that is, infinite essence, and infinite being.

It is not my intention to say much more. For the remaining remarks, which pertain to general metaphysics, I believe, are sufficiently well known. It is not worth while, therefore, to carry the discussion further.

Cogitata Metaphysica,

Part II.

Wherein are briefly explained some points concerning God and His Attributes, and concerning the Human Mind.

Chapter I.

Concerning the Eternity of God.

We have said above that in Nature nothing is given except substance and modes. Therefore it will not be expected that we shall say here anything about substantial forms, or real qualities; for these terms, as well as other similar ones, are plainly inapt. We divide substance into two general heads, namely, Extension and Thought. Thought is either created, the human mind, or uncreated, i. e., God. God's existence we have above demonstrated *a posteriori*, that is, from the idea which we have of God, and *a priori*, or from His essence as the cause of His being. But, although we have already briefly considered His attributes, as the dignity of the argument requires, we will here repeat these and explain them more fully, and at the same time endeavor to answer certain questions bearing upon the subject.

Duration is not assignable to God. The chief attribute, the one to be considered before all others, is the Eternity of God. This term we employ to explain His duration. Or, rather, as we cannot predicate duration of God, we say He is eternal. For, as we noted in the first part of this discussion, duration is an affect of existence not of the essence of things. And since God's existence is His essence, we cannot say that duration belongs to Him. For whoever predicates duration as one of God's attributes differentiates between His existence and His essence. Nevertheless, there are those who ask if God has not existed longer than from the time of Adam, and this seems to them to be perfectly evident since they believe that duration in no way is derived from God. But these persons beg the question; for they assume that God's essence is to be distinguished from His existence. They demand to know whether God, who existed before the creation of Adam, has not existed for a longer time than from the creation to the present. They attribute, therefore, a longer duration to God than to individual objects, as if they suppose that He is continually created by Himself. Did they not distinguish between God's essence and His existence, they would never attribute duration to God, since duration does not correspond to the essence of things. No one would say that the essence of a circle or a triangle, so far as it is eternal truth, has endured for a longer time than from the creation of Adam. Further, since duration is constantly conceived of as greater or less, or as consisting of parts, it clearly follows duration cannot be attributed to God. For as His being is eternal, i. e., there is no past or future to His nature, when we find that we cannot attribute duration to Him we have shown that our concept of God is true. If we attribute duration to God, we separate into parts what is infinite by nature and cannot be conceived except as infinite.

Why some authors attribute duration to God.   The reason some authors attribute duration to God, is: 1. Because they attempt to explain eternity without considering the nature of God; as if eternity could be understood apart from the divine essence, or, indeed, as if it was anything except this. This error

arose from the fact that because of a defective termin-
ology, we have been accustomed to attribute eternity
to things whose essence is different from their existence. As, for example, when we say that the world
has existed from eternity, although this is not implied;
and also that the essence of things is eternal, although
we do not think of the things as even existing.
2. Because they do not attribute duration to things
except so far as they are conceived to be under continual change, and not as we do, only so far as their
essence is to be distinguished from their existence.
3. Finally, because they distinguish between God's
essence and His existence just as in the case of created
objects. These mistakes are at the basis of their error.
The first error was a misapprehension of the nature
of eternity, which was thought to be some form of
duration. In the second, they could not easily distinguish between the duration of created objects and
the eternity of God. Lastly, they distinguished between God's essence and His existence, and attributed
duration to God, as we have said, as though it were
an affect of existence.

What eternity is.   In order to better understand what
eternity really is and why it cannot be
conceived apart from the essence of God, we should
remember what has already been said, viz., that all
created objects or all things except God Himself exist by the power and essence of God, not by virtue of
their own essence. Hence the present existence of
objects is not the cause of their future existence, but
rather the immutability of God. So when we say that
God has created an object we are compelled to believe
that He will conserve it or continue His act of creation. From this we conclude: 1. That created ob-

jects are said to exist because existence is not a part of their essence. We cannot affirm existence of God, for the existence of God is God Himself. So, also, concerning His essence. Hence, while created objects have duration, God does not. 2. Created objects, while they have a present duration and existence, do not have in themselves a future duration or existence, for this must be continually given to them. This, however, is not true of the essence of created objects. Indeed, since His existence and His essence are one, we cannot attribute a future existence to God. For we must attribute to Him now what He has always had. Or, to speak more properly, an infinite existence pertains to God in the same way as an infinite intelligence. This infinite existence I call eternity, This can be attributed to God alone, not to created objects, even though they have no end. So much concerning eternity. I shall say nothing of the necessity of God's being, for after we have demonstrated His existence from His essence this would be useless. Hence we proceed to unity.

CHAPTER II.

Concerning the Unity of God.

We have often wondered at the futile arguments by which some have sought to establish the unity of God. For example, such as the following: " If one being is able to create the world, more than one would be superfluous; and, if all things work toward some end, they must have a common source." Other similar arguments might be mentioned where proof is sought from relative or extrinsic elements. Since such ideas are sometimes held, we shall, in the following order, and as clearly and as briefly as possible, give our demonstration.

God is a single being. Among the attributes of God we enumerate perfect knowledge, and add that His perfection all arises from His own being. But if you say that there are many Gods or perfect beings, all of them must be omniscient. It would not be sufficient for each one merely to know himself. For as each is omniscient he must understand all other beings as well as himself. From which it would follow that the omniscience of each depends partly upon himself and partly upon another. Therefore such a being would not be absolutely perfect. That is, God would not be a being who derives all of his perfection from Himself. But we have already shown that God is in every way perfect and that He exists by virtue of His own power. From which we conclude that God is one being. For if there were many gods it would follow that the absolutely perfect being would have an imperfection, which is absurd. So much concerning the unity of God.

CHAPTER III.

Concerning the greatness of God.

In what sense God is called infinite, in what sense great. We said above that finite or imperfect being cannot be conceived, except we first have some concept of infinite and perfect being, i. e., of God. Therefore God alone can be said to be absolutely infinite, since He alone possesses an infinite perfection. He may be called great, however, or interminable, so far as we think that there is no being able to impose limitations upon Him. From which it follows that the *infinity* of God — an inapt expression — is something essentially positive. For, so far as we conceive Him to be infinite, so far we have reference to His essence or His absolute perfection. The greatness of God is but a relative term; it is not used when we consider God as an absolute or perfect being, but only so far as He is considered as a " first cause." Here, although He may not be perfect except in respect to the creation of the world, nevertheless He is to be considered great. For no being can be conceived, and consequently there is no being more perfect than God by which He can be limited or measured. (Concerning this see Ax. 9, Pt. I.).

What is generally understood by the greatness of God. There are some authors who, when they speak of the greatness of God, seem to attribute quantity to Him. They do this because from this attribute they wish to conclude that God is everywhere present. As if they thought that, were God not in every place He is limited. This is even more apparent in the reasons they adduce to show that God is infinite or great (for they confuse these terms). If God, they say, is *actus purus,* as from necessity He is, He is everywhere present and infinite; for if He is not in every place either He is not able to be wherever He wishes or from necessity (N. B.) He must be moved. From this it is evident that they attribute greatness to God under the concept of quantity. From the properties of extension they look for their arguments for affirming the greatness of God, which is absurd.

God is proven to be everywhere present. If now you ask us how we prove that God is everywhere present, we respond that this has already been clearly proven above, when we showed that nothing could exist even for a single moment unless procreated continually by the power of God.

God's omnipresence cannot be explained. Before we can fully understand the omnipresence of God, we must understand the nature of the divine Will. For by this all things have been created, and are continually preserved. Since this is beyond the limits of human knowledge, it is impossible to explain His omnipresence.

God's greatness sometimes said to be threefold. There are some who think that God's greatness is three-fold, namely, He is great in His essence, in His power, and in His efficacy. But this is nonsense, for they distinguish between God's essence and His power.

God's power is not to be distinguished from his essence. Others affirm the same thing more openly when they say that God is everywhere in power, but not in essence. As if God's power could be distinguished from His other attributes or from His infinite essence, when it is nothing else but this. For if it were anything but this it would either be something created or some accident of the divine essence, without which He could still be conceived. But these suppositions are both absurd. If it were something created it would need God's power to be conserved, and so a progression to infinity would be given. But if it were some accident of His being, God would not be a simple being, which is contrary to what was demonstrated above.

Nor can his
omnipresence.   Finally, by the greatness of His effi-
                    cacy they wish to understand some-
thing beside the essence of God by which all things
are created and conserved. Which is clearly a great
absurdity, and one into which they fall, because they
confuse the divine intellect and the human, and compare God's power with the power of kings.

Chapter IV.

Concerning God's Immutability.

By the term change we here understand all that
variation which can be given, the essence of the object
remaining the same. In general, this signifies the
disintegration of the object, not absolutely, but at
least incipiently; as when we say that turf is changed
into ashes, or that men are changed into beasts. Philosophers have been accustomed to use another term
for signifying this, viz., transformation. But we are
here speaking of a change which is not a transformation, as when we say the rock has changed its color,
character, etc.

                        We must ask now whether there is
Transformation has any changeableness in God. For con-
no place in God.   cerning transformation it is not necessary to say anything more than that God exists necessarily; that is, God cannot be limited in any way, or
be transformed into another God. For as soon as He
is limited there must be other gods, which proposition
we have shown to be absurd.

The causes of   In order that we may understand
change.   more fully what has just been said, we
should remember that all change arises from some

external cause, the subject being willing or unwilling, or from some internal cause, viz., from the choice of the subject itself. For example, men are black, or they grow older and stronger, etc. In the former case the subject is unwilling, in the latter the subject himself desires it. To desire to walk, to show oneself angry, etc., come from internal causes.

God is not changed by any other being. Changes of the former kind, namely, those produced by some external cause, are not found in God, for He alone is the cause of all things, and is not changed by anything He has made. Beside, created objects have in themselves no power of existence, and so much less of causality over other objects. And although in the Scripture it is said that God is angry and sad on account of the sins of men, the effect is here taken for the cause. In the same way we say that the sun is stronger and higher in summer than in winter, although it has not changed its position or increased its power. That such things are often taught in the Sacred Scriptures is seen in Isaiah when he says, ch. 52:2, accusing the people: "Your iniquities have separated you from your God."

Nor even by himself. We continue, then, and ask whether there is any self-caused change in God. This also we at once deny, for all change that arises from volition is made in order that the subject may pass to a better state, which is impossible with a perfect being. Such a change only arises as a means of avoiding something unpleasant or to acquire some good which is wanting. But neither of these conditions is possible with God. Therefore we conclude that God is immutable.[1]

[1] Note.—It will be evident, also, that God is immutable,

It will be noted that I have deliberately omitted the ordinary forms of change, although to some degree we have also considered them. For there is no need to show the impossibility of change in God in respect to every point, since we have demonstrated in Prop. 16, Part I., that God is incorporeal and that these ordinary forms of change apply only to matter.

CHAPTER V.

Concerning the Simplicity of God.

The threefold distinction of things as real, modal, and rational. We proceed to the simplicity of God. In order to correctly understand this attribute of God we should recall what Descartes said in the " Prin. of Phil.," Part I., Arts. 48 and 49, viz., that in nature we know only substances and their modes. From this comes the distinction, Arts. 60, 61, and 62, of things as *real* and *modal,* and *rational.* That is called *real* which distinguishes two substances from one another, whether two different substances, or attributes of the same substance; as for example, thought and extension or different parts of matter. These we know are different because each may be conceived apart from the other, and consequently may so exist. Modal distinctions are of two kinds, namely, that between a mode of a substance and the substance itself, and that between two modes of one substance. The first we recognize because while one mode may be conceived without another, neither can exist apart from the substance whose modes they are; the second be-

when we have shown that His volition and His understanding are the same. This might be proven by other arguments also.

cause while substance can be conceived without its
modes, modes cannot be conceived apart from substance. Finally, a rational distinction is that arising
between substance and its attributes, as, for example,
when duration is distinguished from extension. We
recognize this distinction because substance cannot be
understood without that attribute.

Whence combina-tions arise, and how many forms there are. From these three forms of things
all forms of combination arise. The
first form is that made by the combination of two or more substances, the
attributes being the same, as the combination of bodies,
or the attributes being different, as in man. The second class is made by the union of different modes.
The third is not made in reality, but only conceived
as made in order to better understand objects. What
does not come under the first two of these heads is not
composite, but simple in its nature.

God is not com-posite but simple. From this it may be shown that God
is not composite, but simple being.
For it is a self-evident fact that the
component parts of a composite object are prior in nature to the object itself. Then those substances from
which God is composed are necessarily prior in their
nature to God Himself. Each could then be conceived in itself apart from the concept of God. Each
part, therefore, could exist *per se* and we would have
as many gods as there are substances from which God
is supposed to be composed. For when each part can
exist *per se* it must exist by its own power. Under
these conditions (as we have shown in Prop. 7, Pt.
I., where we demonstrated the existence of God) it
will have the power of giving to itself all the perfection of God. As nothing could be more absurd than

this, we conclude that God is not composite, that is, made by the coalition and union of substances. The same conclusion is also evident from the fact that there are no modes in God's being; for modes arise from the change of substances (vid. *Principles,* Pt. I., Art. 56). Finally, if any one wishes to conceive of some other combination of the essence and of the existence of things, we will not say him nay. Only he should remember that there are not two separate things in God.

The attributes of God are only distinguished by reason. We may conclude, therefore, that all the distinctions we make in regard to the attributes of God are not real but rational distinctions. Let it be understood that such distinctions as I have just made are distinctions of reason, which may be known from the fact that such a substance could not exist without this attribute. Therefore, we conclude that God is simple being. We do not care for the other minor distinctions of the Peripatetics, and proceed, therefore, to the life of God.

Chapter VI.

Concerning the Life of God.

What Philosophers in general understand by life. In order that we may rightly understand this attribute of the life of God, it is necessary that we explain in general what is meant by this term. Here we may examine first the opinion of the Peripatetics. They understood by life the continuance of support to the soul by means of heat (Vid. Aristotle, Bk. I., de Respirat. 8). And, because they had three classes of minds, viz., vegetative, sensative and intellectual, which they attribute to plants, animals and men respectively, it follows that they assume that other objects do not have life. But they did not dare to say that minds and God do not possess life. They feared perhaps lest if they denied life to them they must also deny death as well. Therefore, Aristotle, Metaphysics, Bk. II., chap. 7, gives another definition of life peculiar to minds, namely: "Life is the operation of the intellect." In this sense he attributes life to God who is a cognitive being and is pure activity. We will not be delayed long to refute these conceptions, for what pertains to these three kinds of life which they attribute to plants and animals and men, we have already shown to be mere fiction. For we showed that there is nothing in matter except mechanical form and action. Moreover, what pertains to the life of God relates no more to an act of the understanding than to an act of will or any other faculty. But since I expect no response to what I have said, I pass on and endeavor to explain what life really is.

To what things life may be attributed. Although this term life, by a transference of meaning, is often taken to signify the customs of a people or of an individual, we shall briefly explain its correct philosophical use. It should be noted that if life is attributed to corporeal things, then nothing is void of life; but if only to those objects where spirit is united to body, then only to men or perhaps also to the lower animals, but not to minds or to God. In truth, since the term is a broad one, it should doubtlessly be attributed to corporeal objects, to minds united to, and to minds separated from corporeal body.

What life is in general, and what it is in God. Therefore we will understand by this term life, *the power through which an object preserves its own being.* And although that power in different objects is very different, we still very properly say that those objects have life. Moreover, the power by which God preserves His being is nothing else than His essence. Therefore they speak most truly, who say that God is Life. Nor are there wanting theologians who believe that it was for this very reason that the Jews when they made a vow swore by *living Jehovah,* not by the *life of Jehovah,* as did Joseph when he swore by the life of Pharaoh and said the " *life of Pharaoh.*"

Chapter VII.

Concerning the Understanding of God.

God is omniscient. Among the attributes of God we have enumerated *omniscience* as necessary to His being. For knowledge is an element of perfection, and God, who is in every way perfect, must possess this attribute. Therefore knowledge to the highest degree must be attributed to God, a knowledge so complete that it allows no ignorance or defect of intelligence. Were it not so we would have an imperfection in the attributes of God and so in God Himself. From this it follows that God's knowledge is immediate, and that He does not reason by logical processes.

The objects of God's knowledge are not objects apart from His Being. And further, from God's perfection, it follows that His ideas are not limited like ours to objects apart from Himself. On the contrary, God by

His own power has created objects existing apart from
Himself, but they were determined by His understanding.[1] Otherwise they would have their nature
and essence in themselves and would be by nature
prior to God, which is absurd. Certain ones, because
they have not remembered this, have fallen into egreg-
ious blunders. There are some who think that matter
exists in its own power apart from God, and yet co-
eternal with Him, and that God, knowing this, has
merely set it in a reproducing order and impressed
other forms on it from without. Then others believe
that things are by nature necessary, or impossible, or
contingent, and so far as God knows them as contingent is ignorant whether they exist or not. Finally,
others say that God recognizes contingent being from
its environment because, perchance, He has had a long
experience. Beside these, there are other errors of
like nature, to which I might refer were it not useless
to so do. For from what has been said, the falsity of
these is evident.

But God himself. We revert now to our proposition,
namely, that independent of God there
are no objects of His knowledge, but that He Himself
is the object of His Knowledge, indeed He is that
knowledge. Those who think that the world is the
object of God's knowledge are far less wise than those
who wish some building planned by a great architect
to be considered the object of their knowledge. For
the artificer is compelled to seek for suitable material
outside of himself; but God sought no material out-

---

[1] It clearly follows, therefore, that the understanding of
God by which he knows all created objects, and His will and
power which determined them are one and the same thing.

side of Himself, but things, in essence and in existence, were made by His understanding or will.

In what way God It may be asked, then, whether God
knows sins, dis- knows evil and sin, and distinction of
tinction of
reason, etc. reason, etc. We reply that God necessarily must know those things of which He is the
cause. Especially since nothing can exist for a single
moment except by the concurrence of the divine will.
Therefore, since evil and sin are nothing in things,
but only in the human mind as it compares things
with one another, it follows that God does not know
these independent of the human mind. Distinctions
of reason we have said are only modes of thought,
hence they, too, should be known so far as He conserves the human mind. Not, however, that God has
such modes of thought in order that He may the more
easily retain what He knows. Provided one carefully
attends to these few remarks, there is no question
that can be asked about God's understanding which
cannot easily be answered.

But meanwhile, we must not over-
God's knowledge of look the error of those who think that
universals, and of
particular truths. God knows nothing except eternal
truth, e. g., angels and the heavens
which they think are by nature without beginning and
without end. Beside, in this world nothing but ideas
are without a beginning and unchanging. They seem
to err from choice and to wish to keep up some ob-
scurity. What, indeed, is more absurd than to deny
God's knowledge of individual things, which cannot
exist for a single moment without His sustaining
power! Then they maintain that God is ignorant of
things which actually exist, but knows universals
which do not exist or have any essence apart from

these individual objects. On the contrary, we would attribute to God a complete cognition of individual things, but deny the knowledge of universals except so far as He understands the human mind.

There is but one simple idea in God. Finally, before ending this discussion, it seems necessary to give some answer to those who inquire whether God has many ideas or only one simple idea. To this I respond that the idea of God because of which He is called omniscient is one and simple. For God is called omniscient only because He has an idea of Himself. This idea, or knowledge, since it exists with God, is nothing else than His essence, nor, indeed, could it possibly be anything but this.

What God's knowledge of created objects is. God's cognition of created objects cannot properly be said to be knowledge. For if God so chose, these objects might have some other essence which has no place in His cognition of them. Nevertheless, it is often asked whether His cognition of objects is manifold or simple. To this we would reply, that this question is like those which inquire whether God's decrees and acts of will are one or many; and whether God is omnipresent, or whether His concurrence, by which separate objects are preserved, is the same for all things. Concerning such questions, as I have already said, we have no certain knowledge. Yet, in the same way, we very certainly know that this concurrence of God, if it is correlated with his omnipotence, must be unitary, although its effect is manifested in various ways. So also the voluntary acts and decrees of God (for we may so call His cognition of the world), considered as in God, are not many although through created objects (or better *in* created objects),

they are variously expressed. Finally, if we consider
the analogy of nature as a whole, we are able to consider it as one being, and consequently the idea or
decree of *Natura naturata* will be but one.

CHAPTER VIII.

Concerning God's Will.

We cannot distin-guish between God's essence, His understand-ing by which He knows Himself, and His will by which He loves Himself.
The will of God, by which He
chooses to love Himself, follows necessarily from His understanding, by
which He knows Himself. But we
do not know how His essence and His
understanding, by which he knows Himself, differ
from His will, by which he chooses to love Himself.
Nor does the term *personality*, which theologians use
to explain this, escape our notice. Although we are
not ignorant of the term, we are ignorant of its significance, and unable to form any clear and distinct
concept of its content. Nevertheless, we consistently
believe in the beatific vision of God, which is promised
to faithful ones that this would be revealed to them.

God's will and power considered as objective can-not be distin-guished from His understanding.
As is sufficiently clear from the
preceding, God's will and power considered objectively cannot be distinguished from His understanding.
For we have made it clear that God has not only
decreed that things should exist, but also what character they should have, i. e., their essence and existence
depend upon the will and power of God. From this
we see that God's understanding and power, and will,
by which He created and understands, and conserves

or loves the world, cannot be distinguished from one
another except in respect to our understanding.

*It is improperly
said that God
hates certain
things and loves
others.*   Moreover, when we say that God
holds certain things in disfavor, and
loves others, this is spoken figura-
tively, as when the Scriptures say that the earth shall
bring forth men. That God is not angry with any
one, nor loves any one in the sense that people
ordinarily believe, is evident from the Scriptures
themselves. So Isaiah says, and more clearly the
Apostle to the Romans, chapter 9: "For the children
being not yet born, neither having done any good or
evil, that the purposes of God according to election
might stand, not of works, but of him that calleth,
that the older shall serve the younger, etc." And a
little below: "Therefore, hath he mercy on whom he
will have mercy, and whom he will he hardeneth.
Thou wilt say then unto me: Why doth he yet find
fault? For who hath resisted his will? Nay, but,
O man, who art thou that repliest against God?
Shall the thing formed say to him that formed *it,*
Why hast thou made me thus? Hath not the potter
power over the clay, of the same lump to make one
vessel to honor, and another to dishonor?" etc.

*Why God admon-
ishes men; why
He does not save
them without ad-
monishment; and
why the wicked
are punished.*   If then, you ask: Why, then, does
God admonish men? To this it may
be responded, that God has decreed
from eternity to admonish them at a
given time in order that those whom
He wished to save might be converted.

If you inquire further: Whether God was not able
to save them without this admonishment, we respond
that He was. Why, then, does He not thus save them,
you might inquire. To this I will reply after you

have told me why He did not make the Red Sea passable without a strong east wind, and why He does not make things to move without the agency of other things, and an infinite number of other things which He does by means of mediating causes. Then you will ask: Why are the wicked punished, since, because of their nature, they clearly fulfill the divine decree? I respond that it is also according to the divine decree that they should be punished. And if only those whom we believe to sin from choice should be punished, why do men attempt to exterminate venomous serpents? for they only act according to their nature, nor are they able to do otherwise.

The Scriptures teach nothing which is contrary to the Laws of Nature. Finally, if there are other things which occur in the sacred Scriptures which may be mentioned as points worthy of examination this is not the place to explain them. Here we would merely inquire into those things which we are able to deduce with certainty from Natural Reason, and it is sufficient if we make it evident that the Sacred Pages ought to teach the same things. For truth is not at variance with truth, nor do the Scriptures teach the nonsense that the multitude believe. For if we find anything in them contrary to the laws of Reason we should refute that with the same freedom that we refute such statements in the Koran or the Talmud. However, there is no reason to think that the Sacred Writings contain anything opposed to the Natural Reason.

CHAPTER IX.

Concerning the Power of God.

How we should understand God's omnipotence. We have demonstrated above that God is omnipotent. Here we will only briefly explain in what terms this attribute shall be understood. There are many who discuss this that do not speak with sufficient fullness. They say certain things are possible from God's nature not from His decrees, and that some things are impossible, others necessary. God's omnipotence has a place only in regard to possible things. But we, since we have already shown that *all* things depend absolutely upon the decrees of God, say that He is really omnipotent. And, since we know that He has decreed certain things from His freedom of will and is immutable, we conclude that nothing can happen contrary to His decrees, and that nothing is impossible except that which is opposed to the perfection of God.

All things are necessary in respect to the decrees of God; not some in themselves, and others in respect to these decrees. But perhaps some one will argue that we find some things necessary from the decrees of God and others for some other reason. For example, that Josiah should burn incense upon the altars of the idols of Jeroboam. For if we consider merely the will of Josiah, we will adjudge the thing to be merely possible; nor can it be said to have been necessary in any other sense than that the Prophet had commanded it as being the decree of God. But that the three angles of a triangle are equal to two right angles is self-evident. It is only on account of man's ignorance that these distinctions are made. For if men clearly understood the whole order of Nature they would find all things as determined and as necessary as Mathematics. But as this is beyond human power we conceive some things to be merely possible, others necessary. Therefore, we must either say that God is powerless, since all things are determined, or that He is all powerful, and that all necessity rests upon the decrees of God.

If God had made Nature different, He would have given us other powers of understanding.   If now, it is asked if God had created the world different from its present order, and what is now truth were error, would we still believe the same things to be true? We would if God left our nature as it is. But it would also be possible, if He wished to give us such a nature, as He has indeed done, for us to understand the nature and laws of things just as they are planned by God. Indeed, if we consider God's veracity He ought so to create us. This is also evident from what we have said above, namely, that *Natura naturata* must be considered as unitary. Whence it follows that man is a part of Nature, and ought to be in accord with the world about him. Therefore, from this simplicity of God's decrees it follows that if God had created things in some other way He would have so made us that we would understand them as they were created. So while we desire to retain this distinction which philosophers in general lay down, viz., the *power* of God, we are compelled to explain it differently.

How many kinds of power in God.   We, therefore, divide God's power into two classes. His regulative power, and His absolute power.

God's power is called *absolute* when
What absolute,
what regulative, we consider His omnipotence without
what ordinary
and what regard to His decrees. We call it
extraordinary. *regulative* when we have regard to
His decrees.

We also say God's power is *natural* or *supernatural*.
That is natural by which the world is preserved in its
fixed order. That is called supernatural which causes
something outside of the order of Nature, as for example, all miracles, such as various appearance of
angels, etc. Concerning the latter point there is
evidently some room for doubt. Still it would seem
to be a greater miracle if God should always govern
the world by the same fixed and unchanging laws,
than if at times, on account of the foolishness of men,
He should interrupt the laws and order of Nature
which He from free choice has ordained. (This no
one, except he be mentally blind, can deny.) But we
leave this for theologians to discuss.

Finally, there are some other questions often asked
concerning the power of God: For example, whether
God's power extends to events already past; or
whether He might not have created more objects than
he did? We do not answer these, however, for their
answer is easily seen from what has been said.

CHAPTER X.

Concerning Creation.

It has already been said that God has created the
world. We shall only attempt here, therefore, to explain what is meant by the term *creation,* after which
some opinions on the subject will be carefully examined. We will begin at the beginning.

We say, therefore, that *creation is*
What creation is.   *an operation in which no causes ex-*
cept an efficient one concur. Or, *a created object is*
one which presupposes for its existence nothing
except God.

It should be noted (1) that we have
The ordinary defini- here omitted those words which
tion is rejected.   philosophers insert in their definition,
viz., *ex* nihilo, as if nothing were some matter from
which things are produced. Because they are accustomed to speak in this way, and to think always of
something preceding the given objects, they are not
able, in speaking of creation, to omit this particle *ex.*
The same thing is true concerning matter. Because
all bodies are seen in some position, and surrounded
by other objects, when they are asked where matter
is, they reply, that it is in some imaginary space.
Therefore, it is clear that they do not consider *nothing*
as a mere negation of all reality, but believe or imagine it to be a something real.

2. It should be noted also, that I
The term properly   said in creation no causes concur ex-
explained.   cept one efficient one. I might have
said that creation negates or excludes all causes except
this one. I did not choose to do this, however, lest I
should be compelled to respond to those who ask
whether God had no predetermined end in Himself
for the sake of which He created the world. To make
the definition clearer I added that the created object
presupposes nothing except God. For, if God had
predetermined some end it evidently was not independent of Him, for there is nothing apart from God
by which His decrees are influenced or changed.

Accidents and modes were not created.

3. It follows from this definition that accidents and modes were not created, for they presuppose some created substance beside God.

Time or duration did not exist before creation.

4. Finally, it should be noted that before creation time or duration did not exist, nor can they even be imagined. For time is a measure of duration, or rather it is only a form of thought. Therefore, it not only presupposes the created world, but it depends especially upon human thought. Moreover, duration is limited by the existence of created objects, and hence began when the world began. I say limited by the existence of *created* objects for eternity alone relates to God as we have shown sufficiently above. Hence, duration presupposes that the world has been created or at least that it exists.

It is evident that they who think duration and time existed before the world was created, are laboring under the same prejudice as they who conceive of space apart from matter. So much for the definition of creation.

The work of creating and preserving the world are the same.

There is no need to repeat what is given in Axiom 10, Part I. viz., that no more power is needed to create than to preserve the world. God's work in creating and preserving the world is the same.

Having recalled this point, we proceed to inquire first, what is created and what uncreated, and second, whether what is created has existed from eternity.

What things are created.

To the first inquiry we respond briefly, that everything has been created whose essence is clearly conceived even without existence, and yet is conceived *per se;*

as e. g., matter of which we have a clear and a distinct concept when we conceive it under the attribute extension, whether we think that it exists or not.

How God's knowl-edge differs from ours. But perhaps some one may say that we have clear and distinct knowledge even when the object does not exist, and yet attribute this knowledge to God. To this we reply that we do not say that God's knowledge is like ours, limited by nature, but is pure activity involving existence, as we have shown over and over. For we have shown that God's understanding and will cannot be distinguished from His power or from His essence which involves existence.

Nothing independ-ent of God is co-eternal with Him. Since everything, the essence of which does not involve existence, has been created in its existing form and continually conserved by the power of God, we will not pause to refute the opinion of those who think that the world as chaos, or as matter devoid of form, is co-eternal with God, and so far independent of Him. Therefore we pass on to the second point, and ask whether what has been created could have existed from eternity.

What is meant by the expression from eternity. In order to understand the point just raised we must consider the expression *from eternity*. For we wish to signify by these words something different from the eternity of God. By this expression we now mean duration from the beginning of duration, or such a duration that although numbers were multiplied through thousands of years, and this product again by millions of millions, we would still be unable to express its magnitude.

The world cannot have existed from eternity. It is evident that such duration is impossible; for if the world could have begun at any fixed time then its duration were too short to satisfy these conditions. Therefore, the world cannot have endured from such a beginning to the present. But perhaps you say since God is omnipotent nothing is impossible, and He could have given to the world a duration than which no longer can be conceived. We reply that God, because He is omnipotent, would never have given such a duration to the world. For the very character of duration is that it can always be conceived as greater or less, as in the case of number. You may insist, however, that God has existed from eternity, and since He has perdured all this time there is a duration given, so great that no greater is conceivable. But in this way a duration composed of parts is attributed to God, which idea has been refuted sufficiently when we demonstrated that eternity, not duration, belongs to God. Would that men might remember this! For then they could easily extricate themselves from many arguments and absurdities, and would turn with the greatest delight to the blessed contemplation of God. Nevertheless we proceed to respond to the arguments of those who attempt to show the possibility of such an infinite duration from some fixed time in the past.

Because God is eternal, it does not follow that the things he has created have existed from eternity. In the first place it is said that the thing produced must be co-existent with its cause. And since God has existed from eternity the effects of His being ought to be eternal. This argument is supported by reference to the Son of God, who has existed with the Father from eternity. It is evident that they confuse eternity with duration, and only attribute to God a duration *from* eternity. This is shown, too, in the example cited. The same eternity which they attribute to the Son of God they think can be attributed to created objects. They imagine time and duration to have been instituted before the world began, and think of duration apart from created objects as some think of eternity as independent of God. That both opinions are wrong is now evident. So we respond that it is not true that God was able to communicate His eternity to the world. Neither was the Son of God created, but was eternal like the Father. When we say that the Father had begotten the Son from eternity we only mean that the Father has always shared His eternity with the Son.

In the second place it is argued that *If God acts from* when God acts from choice, He is not *necessity he is not* *infinite in virtue.* less powerful than when He acts from necessity. But if God acts from necessity, since He is infinite in virtue, He must have created the world from eternity. It is easy to reply to this argument if we consider its basis. For these same good men presume that they may hold conflicting ideas concerning a being of infinite virtue. They conceive of God, a being of infinite virtue, as acting both from necessity and from choice. But we deny that God, if He acts from necessity, is a being of infinite virtue. Which action is justified, indeed, and must of necessity be conceded even by those same men when we have shown that a perfect being must be free, and can only be conceived as unitary. Should they reply that it is possible to suppose that God acting from necessity is still infinite in His virtue, we would reply that we are not at liberty to suppose this, any more than we are at liberty to suppose a square circle in order to conclude that all lines drawn from the center to the circumference are not equal. And this, we repeat, is sufficiently proven from what has been said above. We have proven that there is no duration that may not be conceived as greater or less or even double as great. If God acts from free choice it may be created as greater or less. But if God acts from necessity this by no means follows. Under the latter supposition only those things which follow from His nature can be realized, not an infinite number of hypothetical results. Therefore, it may be argued in a few words: If God should create a duration so great that no greater could be given He necessarily diminishes His own power. And this is impossible for His essence and His power are one and the same thing. Therefore, etc., and further, if God acts from necessity, He must have created a duration, than which no greater can be conceived. But had God created such a duration He would not have been of infinite virtue. For we are always able to conceive of a duration greater than the one given. Therefore, if God acts from the necessity of His nature He is not of infinite virtue.

Whence we have a concept of a duration greater than any actually given.
A point which may be a difficulty to some here presents itself, viz., that although the world has only been created some five thousand years, if our chronology is correct, we are nevertheless able to conceive of a much greater duration, and this notwithstanding we have said above that duration depends upon created objects. The difficulty will disappear if we remember that our ideas of duration arise not only as we contemplate created objects, but from reflection upon God's infinite power, in creating them. For we do not think of objects existing *per se,* but only through the infinite power of God. Vid. Prop. 12, Pt. I. and Coroll.

Finally lest we consume too much time with these

futile arguments, but two things need to be kept in mind: (1) The distinction between duration and eternity, and (2) that the former without created objects, and the latter without God are non-intelligible. These things being kept in mind it is easy to answer all these arguments. So we need delay no longer upon this point.

CHAPTER XI.

Concerning the Concurrence of God.

About this attribute of God little or nothing remains to be said after we have shown that each single moment God creates things as if anew. From this we have shown that objects have no power of self determination or of operation in themselves. And this holds true in the human will as well as in all other objects. Then we replied to certain arguments pertaining to this. And, although many other objections are often raised, since these relate more especially to Theology we shall not discuss them here.

Nevertheless, since there are many who admit and believe in this conserving power of God, but in a different sense from us, we shall recall what has already been proven in order that we may detect this fallacy. We have already clearly shown that present time has no connection with future time (Vid. Ax. 10, Pt. I.). Provided we consistently remember this, we shall be able without difficulty to reply to all the objections of these philosophers.

How this conserva-
tion acts in de- But lest we take up this subject
termining things without result we will reply in passing
to act.
to the inquiry whether an additional element of God's

power is needed to begin some action in things. When speaking of motion this same question appeared and we then gave our answer. For we said that God constantly preserves the same amount of motion in nature. If, therefore, we consider the total amount of matter in motion nothing is added. But in respect to particular things there is an additional element given. It does not seem, however, that the same thing can be said of mental phenomena. For it does not appear that they are related the one to the other in this way. Then, finally, since the parts of duration do not have a casual connection, we speak more truly to say then that God continually procreates than to say that he conserves them. Therefore, if man at a particular moment is free to choose some course of action it must be said that God at the present time so creates him. To this it is no objection that the human will is often determined by external influences, and that all nature is inter-related and mutually determining. For this also is so ordained of God. Indeed, nothing determines the will nor does the will determine anything except through the power of God. We confess that we are ignorant of how this may not be opposed to human freedom, or how God can ordain this and still preserve the freedom of man. This we have already admitted.

The ordinary division of the attributes, is more of name than of reality. These are the things I had decided to say concerning the attributes of God. No satisfactory division of them has yet been made. The division given by some, who divide God's attributes into *incommunicable* and *communicable* attributes seems more nominal than real. For the knowledge of God is no more like human knowledge than the Dogstar is like a barking dog, and perhaps it is even less similar.

We would offer this classification:
The classification of There are some attributes which ex-
the author. plain God's essence, and others that tell
nothing of His reality but only explain the modes of
His existence. Of the latter kind are Unity, Eternity,
Necessity, etc.; of the former Understanding, Volition,
Life, Omnipotence, etc. This division is clear and
perspicuous and comprehends all the attributes of God.

Chapter XII.

Concerning the Human Mind.

We pass now to created substance which we classify
as extended and as thinking substance. By the
former we understand matter or corporeal substance.
By thinking substance we understand only human
minds.

Although angels are also created,
Angels are objects
for consideration since they are not known by our nat-
to the Theologian,
not to the Meta- tural powers, they should not be re-
physician. garded in Metaphysics. For their
essence and existence are only known through revelation and so far they pertain only to Theology. Since
the cognition of these beings is so entirely different
from our ordinary form of knowledge the two should
not be confused or classed together. No one should
expect us, therefore, to discuss angels in this connection.

The human mind We turn, therefore, to the human
does not arise by mind concerning which a few things
traduction, but is
created by God; remain to be said. It will be noted
but how, we do
not know. that we say nothing concerning the
time of its creation, for it is not clear just when it is
created since it can exist without the body. But it is

evident that it does not arise by traduction for it would then have a place only in things already created, namely in modes of some substance. But substances, as we have plainly showed above, can be created only by the power of omnipotence.

In what sense the human soul is mortal. We shall add a few words concerning immortality. It is evident that we cannot say of any created object that its nature implies that it cannot be destroyed by the power of God. For he who has the power of creating an object has also the power of destroying it. Beside, as we have sufficiently shown above, no created object has in itself the power to exist, even for a moment, but in every case is continually procreated by God.

In what sense immortal. Although this is all true we all know that we have no concept of a destroyed object, as we have of an object disintegrated or of a generation of modes. For we can conceive clearly enough of the human organism being destroyed but not of the annihilation of its substance. Then philosophy does not inquire what God by His omnipotence is able to do, but seeks to determine from nature itself what laws God has really given to the world. Therefore, what it concludes is rational and fixed it concludes is so from the laws of nature. However we would not deny that God is able to change these laws and all other things as well. Therefore, when speaking of the soul we do not inquire what God is able to do but what follows from the laws of nature.

Its immortality demonstrated. Since it is true, as we have abundantly proven, that substance cannot be destroyed either by its own power, or by the power of any other created substance, unless I am mistaken, it follows that we are compelled to believe from the laws of nature that the soul is immortal. And if we choose to investigate further, we can very clearly demonstrate that it is so. For as we have just shown, it follows from the laws of nature that the mind is immortal. And these laws of nature are the decrees of God, appointed by his will, as we have already made evident. Then beside, these laws are unchangeable. From all of this we conclude with certainty that God has revealed His immutable will concerning man's immortality, not only by revelation, but also by natural reason.

God does not act contrary to, but above Nature, and God is its author. It is no objection to this opinion, if some one should say that at times God sets aside these natural laws in working miracles. For there are many thoughtful theologians who concede that God does not act contrary to, but above the laws of nature. That is, God has many laws of action which He has not made known to man; and these if revealed to man would seem equally natural with the ones he already knows. Therefore it is evident that minds are immortal. I do not see that anything remains to be said concerning its nature. Nor, indeed, concerning its specific functions is there anything to add unless I respond to the argument of certain authors who attempt to show that our sense of perception is not to be accepted as true.

Why some think the will not free. There are some who think they can show that the will is not free but always determined by something from without. They believe this because they think of the will as something distinct from the mind, a substance whose sole nature it is to be indifferent. In order to

remove all confusion on this subject we will explain
the matter in such a way as to easily detect the fallacy
of their arguments.

What the will is. We have said that the human mind
is a thinking object. Whence it fol-
lows that from its nature, and that alone considered,
it is able to do something, viz., to think; that is, to
affirm and to deny. These forms of thought are determined either by something extra-mental or by the
mind itself. But since the mind is a substance itself
whose essence it is to think, it follows that thought can
and should arise from the mind itself. Those mental
acts which know no other cause than the mind itself,
are called *volitions*. And the human mind so far as
it is considered as a sufficient cause for producing these
thoughts is called *Will*.

There is a Will. That the mind, though excited by
no external object has power to act,
is sufficiently proven by the example of the ass of Buri-
danus. For were a man instead of the ass placed in
such a condition of equilibrium he would be regarded
not as a thinking being but as a most stupid ass if he
perished with thirst or hunger. Then this is evident
also from the fact mentioned above, that we have
willed to doubt everything, and not only to hold as
doubtful those things which can be called in question,
but also to expose what is false. (Vid. Principles of
Descartes, Part I. Art. 39).

And it is free. Further, it should be remembered
that, although the mind is influenced
by external objects to affirm or deny, it is not compelled even here but retains its freedom. For nothing
has the power of destroying its essence. What it
affirms or denies it is always free to affirm or to deny

as was shown by Descartes in the fourth Meditation. Therefore, if any one asks why the mind wills this or that, we reply that it is because the mind is a thinking being whose very nature it is to wish, or to affirm or to deny. This is what it means to be a thinking being.

Having stated our position we will *It must not be con-* notice some arguments opposed to *fused with desire.* such a view. (1) Such is the argument: *If the will can choose contrary to the last judgment of the understanding, if it is able to choose contrary to that which is best as determined by the understanding, it is able to choose evil for the sake of its evil. But this conclusion is absurd.* Therefore in the first place it is evident that they do not understand what the will is. They confuse it with the desire the mind has after it affirms or denies something. They were taught this by their teacher who defined the will as *desire for the sake of some good* (appetitum sub ratione boni). We would say on the contrary that the will is *the affirming that this is good or bad,* as we plainly showed when discussing the cause of error, and found that this arises because the will extends further than the understanding. If the mind did not affirm this or that is good, thus exercising its freedom, it would not desire it. Therefore we would reply to this argument by conceding that the mind cannot choose anything contrary to the last judgment of the understanding, that is, it cannot choose anything so far as it is unwilling; as is here supposed when we say that this thing is evil or that the mind does not choose it. But we deny that it is impossible for evil to be chosen or be considered good, for this would be contrary to all experience. For many evil

things are thought to be good and many good things
are considered evil.

2. The second argument is (or the
Nor is it anything, first if you prefer, since the other
except the mind. amounted to nothing): "*If the will is
not determined by the last practical judgment of the
understanding it is self determined. But the will does
not determine itself because in itself and from its nature it is indeterminate.*" From this they proceed to
argue: "*If the will by nature is indifferent to acting
it cannot be determined by itself. That which determines anything must be determined, and that which is
determined must be indeterminate. But the will considered as determining itself would be considered both
as determinate and indeterminate. For these opponents presuppose nothing in the determining will that
is not the same in the will either as determined or as
about to be determined. Nor indeed can anything be
affirmed. Therefore, the will cannot be determined by
itself. But if not by itself then otherwise.*" These
are the words of Professor Heereboordius of Leyden,[1]
in which he clearly shows that he understood by volition not the mind itself, but something else outside of
the mind, a *tabula rasa,* as it were, free from all forms
of thought and capable of receiving images upon itself.
Or rather as a weight in equilibrium, which, as much
as it is determined at all, from without, may be inclined to one side by another weight. Or finally as
something which cannot be understood by the cognition of any mortal. We have just said, and indeed
shown, that the will is nothing but the mind itself.
That is, it is the thinking being, a being who affirms
and denies. So we find when we consider the nature

[1] Vid. ejus Meletemata Philosophica, ed. alt. Lugd. Bat. 1659.

of mind that it has an equal power of affirming and denying. For this, as I have said, is the meaning of thought. We conclude, therefore, that the mind thinks, that it has this power of affirming and of denying. Why then should we seek extra-mental reasons for doing what is sufficiently explained by the nature of the mind itself? But you say, "the mind is not determined more to affirm than to deny; hence some extra-mental cause for volition is necessary." But I argue the contrary; if the mind were by nature only capable of affirming (although such a conception is impossible as long as we conceive of the mind as think- ing being) so that, however many causes concur, it is impossible for it to deny anything. Or if it could neither affirm or deny, it would be able to do neither. Or, finally, if it had the power, as we have shown it has, it would be able to do both from its nature alone, no other cause assisting. This is evidently the case for all who really give to a thinking being the power of thought. Those who separate the attribute of thought from the thing itself from which it is only distinguished by the reason, denude the thinking being of all thought and regard what remains as the funda- mental substance of the Peripatetics. Therefore, I respond that if they understand by will something independent of thought, we will concede that their will is indeterminate. But we deny that the will is something void of understanding; on the other hand, we believe that it is thought, i. e., it is the power of affirming and of denying. Certainly nothing else will satisfy the conditions. Then, too, we deny that even if the will is indeterminate it is therefore de- spoiled of thought, and can be determined by any external object except God's infinite power. For to conceive of a thinking being without thought is the same as to conceive of an extended body without extension.

Why philosophers confuse mind with corporeal things.   Finally, there is no need to consider other arguments, but I shall only say that opponents of this view confuse the mind with corporeal objects because they do not understand the will, or have a clear and a distinct concept of the mind. As has been said, this error arises from the fact that words properly used only to describe corporeal objects have been applied to spiritual things. For they have been accustomed to call those bodies indeterminate which are acted upon by two equivalent external forces acting in opposition to one another. Therefore, since they think that the will is indeterminate they seem to think of it as a body in equilibrium. And, because those bodies have nothing except what they receive from external causes (from which it follows that they are always determined by an external cause), they think that the same thing is true concerning the will. But as we have already made sufficiently clear why these things are so, we shall say no more.

Concerning extended substance we have already spoken sufficiently and beside these two forms of created substance we know no others. What pertains to real accidents and to other qualities has also been sufficiently criticised nor is there need to take any further time in refuting them, so we take our hand from the table.